A Girl Named Maria

From Small Town Italy to Big City America in 1950

As told to Maria's niece

Giuliana Palma

A Girl Named Maria:

From Small Town Italy to Big City America in 1950

By Giuliana Palma

Cover design by Personal Chapters LLC

Unless otherwise noted, all photographs were furnished by Mary or JPIreland Photography

The book cover photo is Maria signing her marriage documents on her wedding day. The signature on the photo is the signature on her passport. The hibiscus is from one of Maria's plants in her front yard. The background color of the book is her favorite color of blue.

Paperback ISBN: 979-8-9927670-7-0

eBook ISBN: 979-8-9927670-9-4

Hardcover ISBN:979-8-9927670-8-7

Library of Congress Control Number: 2026908819

Personal Chapters PUBLISHING

Wakarusa, KS 66546

Dedication

This book is dedicated with love to:

The memory of my grandmother, Maria Michela, who shared her stories with me;

My father Filippo, who lovingly forced me to be brave;

My mother Anna, my first teacher;

My husband Antonio, my hard-working business and life partner.

My brother Giovanni, with me on my American adventure;

My sons, grandchildren and great grandchildren.

Much thanks to the Black Madonna for being with me through it all.

Thank you to Lee Dapp for research help.

Contents

1-Ciao Italia! America Here I Come 9
2-Not What We Expected 17
3-Learning to Cook 23
4-Work. Work. Work 27
5-The Boy Back Home 33
6-My Own Place 43
7-Bristol 49
8-Fighting To Survive 53
9-Success For The Business 59
10-Life With My Boys 63
11-Moiano 67
12-The War 73
13-The House With Grass All Around It 77
14-No Job Too Big Or Too Small 85
15-Changes and Losses 91
16-Not So Golden 97
17-Losing My Husband 103
18-One Thing After Another 109
19-As I Look Back 117
20-I Am Thankful 123
Epilogue 127
Recipes and Kitchen Tips 131
About The Author 143

2014

I T A L Y

Map from ian.mackey.net.

1-Capitolo Uno

Ciao Italia! America Here I Come.

I didn't want to go.

My father told me, "You *will* go to America. You have to go for your brother. If you don't like it, you can come back." He said I could write to him, and he would send me money so I could return home to Italy.

My father, Filippo, was not someone you said no to.

This was 1950, in our small Italian village of Moiano. (That is pronounced *moy on' oh,* with the *moy* rhyming with boy.) Kids did NOT disobey their parents in Moiano. When I was young, there was talk about if you got in trouble, they would put a chain around your neck and throw you in the river. This was said without any humor. That's what it was like.

I really didn't want to go, but I had no choice. My brother and I had to claim our citizenship before we were 21 or we lost the chance to be Americans. My dad wanted us to have the opportunities that came with being American citizens. So, at 20 years old I went. I

(Left to Right) I was leaving my mother, Anna **(also, below)*****; father, Filippo; brother, Roberto and sister, Maddalena.***

Me and Antonio, the boy I left behind.

left my dad, my mother Anna, and my little sister Maddalena. I left my younger brother Roberto, and dozens of cousins. I left my aunts that I felt very close to. I was leaving uncles I really liked, including one uncle who told me I was the best, and now I was going away. I was leaving a boy I had met, Antonio, from a nearby town. I was leaving so much, so much I knew, and going toward so much unknown. I can't form the words to explain how it feels to leave the place you were born, leave your family, go so very far away and never know if you would see them again.

My United States of America passport was number 31, issued in Naples, Italy, on February 8, 1950. The required American Foreign Service Stamp cost $9.00 U.S., which was equal to 5,670 lire back then. The passport was for both of us, my brother and I, so the photo was of us both too. We were United States citizens by birth. We were naturalized citizens. We had it easier than other

Our American passport.

Our passport photo.

immigrants coming to America. They could not refuse us with our U.S. passport. But the passport was only good for four months, expiring on June 8, 1950. That did not leave much time for me to make up my mind about this new country.

I was so mad at my dad. I was mad at Christopher Columbus. Why did he have to discover America? Everyone was crazy to go to America. Everyone but me. People were all excited about me going. That's great. They aren't the one going. They are not responsible for taking care of my brother in a land so far away. If anything bad happens, it will be my fault. If my brother gets into trouble, it will be my fault. My parents had high standards; they expected a lot from us. It felt like it was too much responsibility on my 20-year-old shoulders. The weight was crushing down on me.

I was changing what country I would live in and I had to change a lot of other things too. I was told I had to cut my hair. My long, dark hair was cut shoulder length. I had no say in that or anything else. I had to dress differently. I got a couple of suits. I had never had a suit before. And there were all these instructions about all kinds of things. Do this. Do that. Don't do that. I didn't want to do any of it.

The day came for me to leave. I was heartbroken and scared to death. My parents talked to me for an hour. When it was time to go, I held on to the doorframe, and they had to physically pull me away.

My parents tried to ease my grief. My dad said, "I'm not dead here, you can come back." That was little comfort. I was so scared. My mom gave me a beautiful Italian gold chain with a gold medal of St. Ann. It was like she was having St. Ann look out for me since I would be so far away from her. Mom put it on me the day I left and I have never taken it off in over 70 years. I even shower with it on. Mom was trying to make me feel better with a little bit of home to take with me on my journey.

We left Naples on the Ocean Liner **Vulcania,** ***heading for New York. (Photo from Wikipedia.)***

I cried all the way to the ship, and it was a very long drive. This was my first ride in a vehicle–ever. Naples is a 32-mile journey from Moiano. I had never been anywhere but my own town. The firsts just kept on coming, too. My first ride on a boat was a 4,400 mile trip to America that was supposed to take eight days.

	Series	Roll	Year	Month	Day	Frame	Ship	FHL roll
1	T715	7800	1950	March	01	249	virginia	0
2	T715	7800	1950	March	01	253	pan virginia	0
3	T715	7800	1950	March	02	859	canadian victor	0
4	T715	7802	1950	March	06	540	veragua	0
5	T715	7803	1950	March	08	18	vardefjell	0
6	T715	7803	1950	March	08	33	vila do porto	0
7	T715	7806	1950	March	16	354	haiti victory	0
8	T715	7807	1950	March	19	811	president van buren	0
9	T715	7807	1950	March	00	825	president van buren	0
10	T715	7807	1950	March	20	1220	steel voyager	0
11	T715	7808	1950	March	23	1425	veendam	0
12	T715	7809	1950	March	24	322	kingsport victory	0
13	T715	7809	1950	March	25	620	loide venezuela	0
14	T715	7810	1950	March	27	521	veragua	0
15	T715	7812	1950	March	30	163	new zealand victory	0
16	T715	7812	1950	March	31	588	vulcania	0
17	T715	7812	1950	April	01	943	canadian victor	0
18	T715	7814	1950	April	04	118	vibeke maersk	0
19	T715	7815	1950	April	07	643	vernicos nicolaos	0
20	T715	7815	1950	April	08	841	algonquin victory	0
21	T715	7815	1950	April	08	940	willamette victory	0
22	T715	7817	1950	April	13	1433	valacia	0
23	T715	7818	1950	April	15	787	volendam	0
24	T715	7819	1950	April	17	228	san venancio	0
25	T715	7819	1950	April	17	307	veragua	0
26	T715	7820	1950	April	19	5	veendam	0
27	T715	7820	1950	April	20	473	foundation vera	0
28	T715	7820	1950	April	20	727	vergelegen	0
29	T715	7823	1950	April	25	10	haiti victory	0

Entries 1 to 29 out of 29

The ships registry in New York showing all the ships arriving in March, 1950. (Thanks to Family History Library.)

We sailed on the Vulcania on March 20, 1950. It was an Italian ocean liner with a capacity for 1,760 passengers. During the war, this ship had spent 2½ years as a United States troopship. Now it was taking me and my brother to the United States. Rough seas extended our voyage until March 31. That was bad luck for me. I was sick to my stomach the entire time. I was throwing up every minute on that stupid boat that I did not want to be on in the first place. I ate nothing and I was still sick. The only thing that even sounded good were lemons. My brother spent all my money and the last two dollars of his money on lemons for me. I would just suck on the lemon for the juice.

My brother was ok. The ship didn't bother him. At least that was good. This nice, older Italian woman encouraged me to go up on deck and get a little fresh air one day. I started up, but when I went past the kitchen, the smell of food made me start throwing up again. So back down I went and laid down.

We were second-class passengers so we were on one of the lower levels of the ship. I was in a cabin with three girls from Palermo, Italy. I had never been to Palermo; it was about 470 miles south of Moiano. These girls were from my country, but I couldn't understand them. They were talking to each other, and their dialect of Italian was very different from mine. I thought to myself, *Great, I don't even understand Italians from Palermo, and I am going to America and I know NO English!* I was even madder at Christopher Columbus and my dad. I felt so alone.

We finally landed in New York, USA. The boat spilled us out into this big place. Ellis Island looked like a very big garage with nothing but walls and lots of people of all ages. The officials asked us our names and without checking with us to see if it was ok, they translated them into "American" names. Maria became Mary… Giovanni became John.

Customs went through our possessions and took our two big bottles of olive oil, prosciutto, cheese, all the food our mom had sent with us. Someone there was eating good that night, but it wouldn't be us.

Our Uncle Joe, whom we had never met, picked us up. He had been sent a picture of us so he knew what we looked like. We had no picture of him. We were told to wait in the big hall by the water for our name to be called. Dad had told me his sister would treat me like a queen in America and that she loved us. They would help us in our new country. I was looking forward to their help. I needed their help. When Dad was in America, he had helped them financially and emotionally. When my uncle lost his job, my dad supported their family. When my aunt lost a child, it was her brother, my dad, who helped her build up strength coming home from work with beef steak for her. It was too expensive for everyone, so he bought just enough for her. Now it was their turn to repay his favors, to us, his kids. That is what I was told.

I believe my father made two trips to the U.S. and spent about three years on each trip. This man from the little town of Moiano was in Susquehanna, Pennsylvania working on the railroad.

My father's American passport that he was so proud of and a photo of him later in life.

A map showing Moiano, Sant'Agata and Naples. I had only ever been in Moiano. (Map from Bing.)

When he was laid off from the railroad, he got a job working for General Electric. All this time he was sending money home to my mom in Italy. He thought it was so funny that Pennsylvania was abbreviated Pa…like half of *papa* or father in Italian. In his free time, he worked on getting his U.S. citizenship. Dad went the first time, and they told him to come back when he had learned some more English. So, he kept studying English and going back until he achieved his goal of U.S. citizenship and got a U.S. Passport on March 2, 1928. When he came to America the first time, it was with his Italian passport. His second trip to the U.S.A. he was an American with his own American passport. He was very proud of his dual citizenship. That was the citizenship he had achieved for us. That is why we were here in America, to claim what he had worked for, for himself and for us, as long as we went before we were 21.

2 – Capitolo Due

Not What We Expected.

We lived with my Uncle Joe and Aunt Maddalena and their four kids in Binghamton, New York for about a year. Then we moved with them to Johnson City, New York. Uncle Joe was my mom's cousin and Aunt Maddalena was my dad's sister. Their kids, our four cousins, were all older than us. I hoped they would be nice to us and help us get used to life in our new country … you know, take us out with them, introduce us to their friends. I expected they would treat me the way I would have treated anyone, especially my cousins, in that situation. But that did not happen.

We were looked upon by them all as hired help that they didn't have to pay. Life with them was not as expected. We helped my aunt and uncle and their kids more than they helped us. That is the truth.

We had to pay them for room and board. I worked all day. Then I came home and worked all evening doing the cooking, cleaning and laundry…and got to pay them for the privilege. We were slaves. I wouldn't treat a stranger that way, let alone a blood relative! My uncle tried to help us. He bought us a book about learning English but it mysteriously disappeared. When I asked him about the book, he just shrugged his shoulders as if to say he was sorry. We were told we had to pay my aunt's friend to learn English. She was not much help. We would go to her house, pay her, and she would be taking care of her own kids with little time to help us.

All the English my brother and I learned was self-taught. This was a good example of how everything, even how we spent our money, was controlled by my aunt. Though my aunt and uncle took the newspaper, we were not allowed to look at it. Great care was taken to be sure it was hidden away so we couldn't. How could they be like this to us? My Mom used to tell me things could always be worse. At this time in my life, I wondered how it could possibly be worse.

I was making Lipton soup for my brother and me. The right way to do it is to boil the pasta in one pan to keep all the extra starch from being in your soup. A second pan was where I made the soup. My aunt forbid me from using two pans, saying it was wasteful, I was using too much gas. We were helping to pay for the gas, and I was the one washing the pans. What a contrast from when I cooked for her and her immediate family. When I was doing their cooking, there was no limit to the number of pans I could use or how much gas I could use. According to my aunt, her son had a delicate stomach and required a special diet. I had to make food for the others and separate, special things for him too, and then food for my brother and me. Not only was my aunt telling me what I could and couldn't do, but her kids, my cousins, bossed me around. I was told "what are you unhappy about? If you were in Italy, you would be working." I know I wouldn't have been treated the way they were treating me. I was like Cinderella.

There were six kids in the house but only two, my brother and I, were doing all the work. I will never forget getting all my work done one Sunday night and my boy cousin, the one I made special food for, told me to go polish the copper. I told him I did it yesterday, but he insisted. I had to do it again. Many years later, this cousin would write me a letter asking me to please forgive him. He was sorry he had treated me this way. So you know what I am saying is true, and it was really bad for him to have written an apology all those years later.

One of his sisters would take our paychecks to the bank where she worked and cash them. They completely controlled where and how we spent our money. She would take out a payment for

My brother John and I with a couple of young relatives.

my dad (to repay him for what he borrowed to send us here), take out room and board charges and bring back to us the little bit that was left. When you are getting paid 35 cents an hour, it was not a big check to begin with. Part of our money was sent to the other girl cousin who was away at school. We helped pay for that cousin's college, but we had so little ourselves. For example, my brother brought home a couple of nice, clean, cardboard boxes from the factory. He cut extra cardboard and made compartments in the box for socks, underwear and shirts. Then he put it in the closet. It was his bureau and chest of drawers. If we were home in Italy, we would have had a chest of drawers. It would have been so much better for us there.

My dad had worked so hard and thought he had paved the way for us. He had prepared a plan for us by helping his sister and her family. When we came to America, they were going to help us, he said. My dad was an honest man, and he really believed it would be good for us. He never dreamed it would be like this. I know that. It wasn't his fault that we were being mistreated. It wasn't his fault I felt trapped. I saw no way to improve my situation besides waiting it out.

My plan was to save money and learn more English. Then we would make a move. I didn't want to worry my parents by telling them how bad we were being treated. I was embarrassed to tell anyone. If I complained to my dad, he would be disappointed. My aunt told me if I didn't do what she said, she would write my dad. I was worried that he might believe his sister over me. One time back home an adult told my parents that I was seen with a boy (how's that for strict – just seen with a boy) at *Festa* evening Mass. It wasn't me. It was the friend I was usually with, Peppinella, who was the same height and age as me. My parents believed the adult and came looking for me. Luckily, I had fallen asleep and hadn't left the house. That's the only way I got out of being in trouble.

From Italy, my parents could not see for themselves, so I didn't feel confident they would believe me. It *was* hard to believe that my aunt and cousins would mistreat us like they did. I was especially worried about my mom being upset. My Nonna and my mom always told me to "do good and forget…do bad and think about it." So, I was trying to do good and not worry them. My mom and Nonna couldn't even picture what life was like here because they had never visited America. I did not want them to worry. Besides, there was nothing they could do from Italy anyway.

I could have gone back home to escape this situation. But I was embarrassed to go home, because everyone wanted to come to America. I thought, *If I go back, people won't understand and they will think I am ungrateful. Dad spent so much to send us here, he even had to borrow some of the money.* I decided the best plan was to save what I could and pay for my own way home. I didn't want to bother anyone.

I worked and worked, trying to save up enough money to go back. I started an account at the credit union my uncle recommended, going there to make deposits whenever I could. Waiting in line to make my deposit, people around me were talking to each other but no one was speaking anything I could understand. They sounded like a bunch of sheep…baaa baaa baaa. Such a strange sound coming out of people, baaa baaa baaa. One time the bank tellers were trying to get me to help them communicate with another person in line. They wanted me to translate for her. How funny! She was definitely not speaking Italian. I think it was Polish. That was one more language I did *not* speak.

The first job my brother and I had was picking beans, along with a flatbed truck full of immigrants. The truck would pull up, and as many as could fit in would climb on and the truck would take us out to the bean field and dump us. We did this every day, all summer long, for 50 cents a bushel. Yes, you heard me right. A BUSHEL! That is a lot of work for 50 cents. The minimum wage in 1950 was 75 cents an hour. We didn't even get minimum wage per hour. Instead, we got paid by the bushel.

It was a long summer. My cousins never worked like this. I couldn't help but wonder where all the money and gold in the streets was if we had to do this. The stories back home were of so much wealth in America that there was money and gold in the streets. Life was supposed to be so much easier, and our futures automatically filled with success once we arrived on America's shores. That is what people in my hometown believed. That is why everyone was crazy to go to the United States. The real story, the real welcome to America, was picking bushels of beans for 50 cents each. If I was still in Italy, it would have been better than this.

3 – Capitolo Tre

Learning To Cook.

A restaurant in Schenectady hired me to work in their kitchen. It was opened in 1947 by people from Italy. When I was there, they did a good business. It was close to the General Electric Factory so we had a lot of businessmen who ate regularly with us. We would have retirement parties in the basement and all the big bosses at G.E. would be there. This restaurant had a reputation for good food, and nothing was cheap.

Working there I had the experience of people coming into the kitchen to tell me they liked my cooking. The first time it happened, a man was handing me a $20 bill, and I asked him what that was for. He said, "You made the chicken I ate, and it was real good. This is a tip." There were several older Italian men who would do that. They liked what I had made for them and after that they started asking for me. Other people who worked at the restaurant were jealous of me because of this. They shouldn't have been. They still got their tips. There were two sisters-in-law who were servers who were especially upset. This was the first time I had been noticed for my skills in the kitchen.

I left home so young that most of what I learned about cooking was learned here at this restaurant. It was a large kitchen with a big menu, and I had to be able to do it all. There was always a pot boiling on the stove. I became a very good cook. I could make anything Italian–spaghetti, lasagna, veal, chicken, fish. I've been told my "American" cooking is very good too.

I was asked why I liked to cook so much and I said it is because I liked to eat. And I liked to eat good food. People used to tease my husband about not wanting to go out to eat. He said, "Why should

I go out to eat when I have the very best food at home."

Growing up in Italy during the war, there were rations, especially for meat. And I really liked meat. There was no shortage of meat in America. I liked fixing chicken because you can make it so many different ways. I would pound it flat and then roll it up with filling or spices or roast it like a turkey and slice it with gravy. There are so many things you could do with a chicken. I liked making *lasagna* for company. I could make it ahead of time, and it would stay good for the gathering. When I made sauce, (see recipes in the last section of the book.) I would make a giant pot. I would start early and let it simmer all day. Then I canned it in Mason jars, so I had sauce for many meals to come.

I would go to the butcher and have him slice steak very thin, like for *scaloppini* for my *brasciole*. I would buy a big pork roast and a big beef roast and grind the meat at home to make meatballs. I bought Italian sausage, boiled it, then browned it in olive oil. At home I would freeze enough meatballs, sausage and *brasciole* for one meal in food saver vacuum bags and stock up my freezer. Then all I had to do was open a jar of sauce, thaw the meat in the sauce, boil some pasta and we were set, even at the last minute.

My freezer always had several pounds of home-made *cavatelli* noodles. I made a lot at a time because they were a lot of work. Back at the restaurant we made them by hand, which I continued to do most of my life. A retiree of G.E., who then worked at the restaurant made me my very own big wooden board for making bread and pasta. I still have it. There is a machine that makes *cavatelli* noodles now and I have used that method too.

I liked to make big pots of homemade soups. For chicken noodle soup, I would put four whole chickens and a beef bone in a big stock pot. Then I tied celery and parsley together and dangled it on the side of the pot. I did this especially when someone was sick. Then I would freeze extra servings of the soup to have on hand.

Because of the war and the way my family was, I never wasted food. The restaurant never wasted food either, so we got along well. If you have done without food ever in your life, that is something you remember. It stays with you always.

This is a picture of me.

4 – Capitolo Quattro
Work, Work, Work.

After the restaurant, I worked at a glove factory until it closed. Next, I worked for the Michael Company, which made parts for televisions. My job on the assembly line had me on a punch press. I would stomp down with force on this metal thing with my heel for eight hours a day. They would give me a big sheet of plastic, and I was to punch out as many of these shapes as I could. There was a supervisor watching us to be sure we didn't waste any of the plastic. We had to get the maximum number of punches possible.

It was a painful and very physical job. I broke a deep vein in my knee, plus my heel and ankle would regularly swell up. To this day, I have problems with my veins and ankles. The circulation is not good in my legs, and my feet feel like they are in an ice block. This is a permanent reminder of my injuries working on the punch press.

My brother and I both worked at the Endicott Johnson factory making shoes. I used a sewing machine and was in a three-month probationary period at first. If I wanted to stay employed, I had to reach my quota. They would give me a dozen shoes at a time and then

The archway announcing the place my brother John and I worked. (Photo from Wikipedia.)

my pay was decided by how many dozen I completed. It was an assembly line and each day you got your assignment. For me it was usually stitching one element of the shoe or putting the heel on and covering the heel with the leather. There was no union at this factory. We were told not to talk to the union people or we would be fired. Pretty funny. I couldn't have talked to them even if I wanted to. When a needle broke, I didn't know what to call it in English. I just took the broken needle out of the sewing machine, took it to them and they gave me another one. I did the same thing with thread. I took the empty spool to them, and they gave me another spool.

It was every person for themselves at the shoe factory. All the other women working in this area were a lot older than me and had been there a while. I was the very motivated new person trying my best to meet my quota. I did really well and they gave me a raise. I was happy about that, but they told me to slow down because I was making all the other workers mad. The other women all turned on me. It was not a good environment. This was probably my favorite job though. That is because the bosses were fair. At the end of the year, they gave us a profit-sharing bonus that was about $200. That was a lot of money back then. When I left to get married, they told me they would save me a job, even though I would be gone a month. That was nice of them.

After leaving my paid job, I would go to my aunt and uncle's and work into the night there cooking, making homemade macaroni and doing the dishes afterwards. On the weekends I cleaned other houses for extra money. I never would have been cleaning people's houses in Italy. I had no days off, barely any hours off.

My brother kept telling me I better get out of my aunt and uncle's house before they killed me. My brother had a big mouth. I told him not to, but he wrote a letter home telling my parents to get me out of there before they killed me. I never mentioned the mistreatment to my dad because I did not want to worry them.

This is me.

The aunt of a friend of mine went to Italy, and I sent gifts for her to give my mom and dad. When she returned, she asked me why my mom was so worried about me. It was that letter my brother sent. I knew he did it because he cared about me, but he had ruined my credibility with our parents.

I continued to write my dad every week. Every week he wrote me back. He was a good letter writer. In Dad's letters he talked about a lot of things, but he never mentioned the Italian boy, Antonio, who had been coming over to the house to see me. Funny, huh? My dad would read my letters to my mom because she could not read or write. Her generation of Italian women did not get to go to school like I did.

My brother, John, was supposed to shovel coal, empty the ashes, shovel snow and other things. He argued with my aunt about this, wondering why her son (the one I had to make special food for) couldn't do it or at least help. This caused trouble for us both. Even though I was the one doing most of the work, my brother said he couldn't take it anymore. He suggested we move in with a Polish guy he had met at work. I was scared. What if I was there sometimes without my brother? I did not know this guy at all. What if he was like the horrible people my aunt kept warning me about? My brother said the guy was going to charge us a lot less. We would only pay half as much as my aunt was charging us. Best of all, nobody would bother us or tell us what to do. But I didn't know him. He was a stranger. I reasoned that if our relatives treated us this bad, wouldn't a stranger be even worse? I was too scared to go. It sounded too good to be true. I told my brother "I may be dying here, but I'm not going there. We need to wait a little more time and then move out." I felt bad for him, but I couldn't do anything about the situation until we saved up some more money.

My brother came to visit after he joined the U.S. Air Force.

Since I wouldn't go, he joined the U.S. Air Force and left. Now I was worried about something happening to him in the service. He was so young. He knew so little English. That scared me. He could get hurt or get in with the wrong kind of people. I was his legal guardian. If something happened to him, I would feel like I did not do what my father had asked of me. I was told to take care of my younger brother. I took that seriously. My parents trusted me to do that and I did not want to let them down. I did not want to be blamed for any harm coming to him.

I had nightmares about breaking the news to my parents that something bad had happened to my brother. The U.S. Air Force got a good man, and he got out of a bad living arrangement, but I was still there. After he left, it was really lonely. I loved my brother. I really did not want to lose him. My situation was bad but at least he had been there with me. I felt like he had deserted me. I was really all alone now.

My brother got his naturalization papers completed in the Air Force. I had to go to the American Embassy in Syracuse, New York, for an oral test with eleven questions. I sure wished my brother was with me. I was so scared, I couldn't eat or drink, I was that nervous! What if I failed? What if I forgot the right answers?

What if I didn't understand what they meant? They asked questions about whether I would defend America, what nation did I pledge my loyalty to, things like that, along with some history questions. At the end of the day, I could not keep my shoes on. It was like I had shrunk with all that nervous energy; like I lost weight just from the stress and worry.

I passed the test. Now I was officially a naturalized American with papers to prove it.

5 - Capitolo Cinque

The Boy Back Home.

After my trip to Syracuse, I was especially tired, but I would fall into bed exhausted every night. Many times, I cried myself to sleep. I didn't have anyone to talk to. I would think of my real home, wishing I was back there. I thought of Antonio. He was from Sant' Agata De' Goti, a town that was about five miles away from Moiano, reached by weaving around through the mountains.

We wrote letters back and forth every two weeks. He said nice things in his letters. He had been after me for a while at home. For about three months before I left, Antonio would ride his bike that five miles to my house once a week. He would spend a couple hours with me and ALL the rest of the family. That was the way it was done in Italy.

I was told by my father that if I brought someone home, I must marry him. I had never brought anyone home. Now this guy was coming to my home, but I didn't bring him! Maria Michela, my grandma (Nonna) liked him. My mom said he was arrogant, but that was the only thing she didn't like. She didn't think anyone was good enough for her girls. My sister really liked him too, and after we left, she would walk the five miles to visit his mother. My mom's brother said he was a nice guy and was healthy, and he was kind with sheep and animals. He thought that was a good sign, his kindness to animals. Antonio's father had died when he was young and he was sent up the mountain to live with his uncle. He would help tend the sheep and watch over his uncle's other animals. When Antonio was old enough, he could get his own animals, his uncle had told him.

The rest of the people in Moiano wanted me to marry a boy from

The map shows the route Antonio had to walk or ride his bike to come see me. The quickest walk was an hour and 36 minutes. No one had cars back then. (Map from Bing)

Moiano. They chased him out of town. One of my cousins tried to cause an accident to get him to leave and stay away. Antonio hurt his leg but still kept coming back. I told Antonio that I was leaving for America, and I didn't want to get involved with him. I didn't believe he would come with me anyway, or that I would ever return to Italy. My life plans were all being made by someone other than me. If it was up to me, I wouldn't have left Italy. He told me he was going in the Italian Army, but when he got out, he would come to America. I

Antonio in his Italian Army uniform.

told him he could only come if I sent for him. He said, "Whatever you want to do, I'll do." That sounded good. (I haven't heard that from him again in our 66 years of marriage. How things change after you marry!)

I thought at least with an Italian boy, I would know his language. The worst thing about coming to America was that I couldn't talk. It was such a disadvantage. With Antonio we would be able to speak Italian and understand each other as we learned more English. Surely that would give us less chance of divorce, being able to talk to each other. I would also have some idea of who I was marrying because I knew his background and family.

Antonio was the only boy I had even talked to. I had no one to compare him with. There were boys who were better looking, but Antonio had a sense of pride and honor. I thought those were good qualities. I hoped our similar Italian backgrounds would make for a good marriage. Before I left home my Nonna made me promise that I would come back to Moiano to get married. That also made me lean toward Antonio, the only Italian boy I had ever talked to. If my cousins were an example of the way people lived in America, I didn't want to be like them. I didn't like the way they lived here. Also, my aunt I lived with told me scary stories about American men. She said you could not trust people; they came to the door and would kill you.

So, the idea of trying to date American men was sure not appealing.

I had never been on a date in my life. In Italy, if I had gone out, I would have had to have a brother or male cousin go with me. That was impossible in my current situation with my aunt and uncle. My aunt did her best to frighten me, and she was successful. She wanted me to stay forever and work for her. But on that she was unsuccessful, and it became another reason to get married. It was a respectable way to get away from that horrible situation with my aunt. She was sure mad when I moved out. She told me she would give me my wedding gift after I returned from Italy. I never even received a card, let alone a gift.

I took a month's leave of absence from my job and went home to get married. It was 1952. I was 23 years old. I had planned my wedding at the time of the year when our town had our *festa.* This was the time people came home to Moiano. The whole town celebrates *Madonna della Libera,* a beautiful work of art. We affectionately call her our Black Madonna. We looked upon her as the patron saint of San Pietro Apostolo Church. All my life I have prayed to the Black Madonna. In my home today I honor her still with a large picture of her in my bedroom. Praying to her makes me feel calmer. I have looked to her all my life. I was going to get married *AND* visit the town at the time that it was best to be home. My parents would be proud that I was home then.

An original painting of The Black Madonna by artist Noemi Lamela, a gift from my niece Jeanmarie. This niece was named for me.

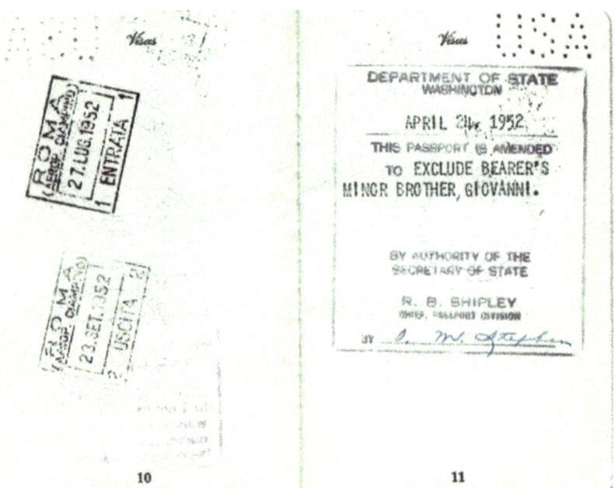

Changes made to my passport when I returned home to Italy to get married, excluding my minor brother.

My passport was renewed and amended to exclude "bearer's

minor brother, Giovanni." They just drew an X on my brother's face to take him off. It would now be valid until October 23, 1952. I had saved up enough money for my flights to and from home. No way I was going on any boat, ever again!

I had also saved enough money to buy my wedding dress, shoes, gloves–everything I needed for my wedding. I mailed it all home to Italy ahead of my trip. It was all there when I got home. Women didn't travel alone in those days, so my Uncle Joe escorted me home.

Weddings in Italy are a serious affair. Mine sure was. Looking at the wedding pictures, I cannot find a single smile anywhere, on anyone. Bride. Groom. Relatives. Sober looking faces. Much different than American weddings and American wedding pictures where everyone is smiling big smiles.

My wedding pictures were very serious. Left to Right: Uncle Antonio, brother Roberto, my mother's brother-in-law, Uncle Joe (my escort home), my mother's cousin, my father, myself and my husband.

It didn't help that one of my aunts wanted me to marry her son, my cousin, so he could come to the United States. That's how desperate people were to come to America. I told her she may have lost her mind, but I sure hadn't. I got married to Antonio in the church just down the street from my childhood home with the statue of the Black Madonna looking down on me. This is my church. The church I was baptized in, made my first communion in, had my confirmation in. Now I was getting married here. My family has attended Mass here for centuries. My Nonna was married there so long ago, and my great niece in Italy was married there recently.

This is me signing the marriage paperwork on my wedding day.

It is a beautiful church built in the eighteenth century with a bell tower about 30 meters high. To this day, seeing pictures of the church makes me feel good and makes me smile. Unlike the wedding pictures. They do not make me smile and it was obvious I was not happy. That kiss in the wedding ceremony was our very first, and it was witnessed by a church full of people.

My husband and I had no honeymoon and were reunited six months later.

After the wedding, Antonio went to his home to sleep, and I went home to my parents' house to sleep. We couldn't even say goodbye privately. In Italy it is good luck when it rains on your wedding day. When we came out after the wedding, it was raining. I hoped that saying was true. I was not sure what would happen next. I was worried about my marriage, and there was much to do.

I got my passport amended again on September 18, adding my

married name. I really was American now. Italian women do not take their husband's last name in Italy. I arrived back in the U.S.A. on September 24, 1952, with my husband's name but without my husband. No honeymoon for us.

"Ciao, ora siamo sposati. Ci vediamo a sei mesi. Arrivederci!" This translates to "Hi, we are now married. See you in six months. Goodbye."

Before we got married, I had told Antonio what it was like in America. I told him it was not easy. I told him he didn't have to get married. I wanted to be totally honest with him. So many people had unrealistic ideas of what things were like in the U.S. Antonio knew very few people could go and he wanted to be one of them. He still wanted to get married. Even though people in my hometown, including my mother, had told him I would not be coming back for him.

I figured I was ahead of him on what I knew, so he would be working hard to catch up with me. I trusted him to learn like I did. That would keep him busy and on track. He was leaving his mom, aunt and two sisters, who had all spoiled him rotten. I was worried about that. I was afraid to talk to Antonio's mom. She looked mean. I knew she was not happy that he was going to move to America with me and leave her. Back in the U.S., I had so much paperwork to fill out and file so Antonio could join me in the U.S. They checked back seven generations in his family to make sure there were no criminals. Antonio also had to pass a health check examination.

After all of that and the mountain of paperwork was done, I still had to prove that I had $1,500 in the bank, a job for Antonio, and a place for us both to live before he could come. I got Antonio a job helping a builder that my uncle knew. That was sure a better job than my first job in the U.S. Thinking back, it is amazing all I did. It sure was not an easy thing to do for anyone, let alone

Antonio finally joins me in America.

a woman in 1952, especially a woman whose native language is Italian.

In March of 1953 my 24-year-old husband Antonio became Tony as he arrived in America aboard the Andrea Doria. This ship is famous, but not for bringing my husband over. It collided with a Swedish ocean liner three years later and sank. Tony said it was a sign he should never go back to Italy. Such a funny guy!

When I came back from getting married, I lived with Uncle Angelo and Aunt Antoniella, another aunt and uncle in Schenectady, New York. Uncle Angelo was my mom's brother and Aunt Antoniella was my dad's cousin. I was glad to be out of the last living situation where I had stayed in a closet under the steps with a small rollaway bed. There was no window at my other aunt's, and the only place for any clothes was an over-the-door hanger. This was a better living situation, with a small bedroom for my husband and me.

I remember my husband wanted me to lay out his clothes on the bed each morning. He told me his sister and his mom used to do that for him. But I had more than enough to do. I told him they were not here, so he would have to do it himself. But I did set out his clothes when it was something special so I was sure he would look nice.

While living with them, I had to cook and clean for my aunt, uncle and cousins. Every weekend two daughters and one son would come over, and they had three or four kids each. I had to cook for them too. On top of that, I was required to pay for half of all the grocery costs. That was for everyone, including all the relatives who came every weekend. We were asked to pay half of the taxes on their house too, but thankfully, my uncle would not take it.

I wanted a place of my own.

Working in the kitchen at my aunt's house as she watches.

6-Capitolo Sei

My Own Place.

Tony worked at the job I had gotten him for six months. He made $32 a week. I was making $14 a week. Then he had an uncle move to Pennsylvania. He was really a good guy. This was nice, as my husband's father had died when he was six years old. We both liked having his uncle around.

Tony got a job in Philadelphia at a body shop, thanks to his uncle's son-in-law. We moved and finally had a place of our own. It was an upstairs apartment on Fuller Street. There were lots of young people our age living there and it was across the street from Tony's cousin. That was so good, especially when I became pregnant. We shared the same doctors and then the same baby doctor, too.

I welcomed my beautiful 8 lb. 7 oz. baby boy Vincent in October of 1955. I was so happy, but also sad, as I couldn't share any of this with my mom, sister or my aunts in Italy. This was back when long-distance calls were so expensive that they were rarely done. Pictures were

Our first place of our own, an upstairs apartment on Fuller Street.

expensive too. All I could do was write letters to my dad to share with my mom and sister about my baby boy. I would have liked for my son to grow up with lots of relatives close by, just the way I had. But that was not to be.

I would pack Tony a lunch each morning and he would go to his job. They were paying him a small salary but had promised a raise after a certain period of time. When that time came, Tony went to his boss and said, “Where is my raise?” The guy laughed in his face and said, “You can’t go nowhere. You can’t talk.” Tony told him he quit and walked out the door.

He came home that night and didn’t say a word to me about any of this. The next day, I packed his lunch and Tony left just like he had before. But instead of going to his job, he was going out looking for work. I had no clue what was going on until I got a phone call for Tony. I told the caller he wasn’t there. He asked where he was and I told him he was at work. The guy said “This is his work. He quit over a week ago, but we want him to come back.”

When Tony came home, I asked him how work had been. He said it was as usual. Then I told him about the phone call. I couldn’t believe he had not told me he had quit. There I was, making his lunches for over a week, and thinking all was well. His strategy worked though, and he got the raise they had promised him.

We had to fight to be treated well and Tony had won his first American battle.

Vince was a good baby, but he didn’t want to sleep at night. I would walk back and forth in my bare feet as quietly as possible trying to get him to sleep. The older lady who lived downstairs said, “Honey, don’t you believe in sleeping at night? I hear you walking on the floor all night long!” I told her she could either hear me walking or my baby crying. Those were the two choices.

She was not the easiest person to rent from. We had no clothes dryer back then but were not allowed to hang laundry outside. She said her husband didn't like seeing rags on the line. The building had a clean basement, so I took my wringer washer to the basement and washed our clothes and all Vincent's diapers there. We put up a clothesline in the basement and that is where I hung my clean laundry. One time the basement door was locked, and I had to have diapers for my baby. (Remember, now, that this was before disposable diapers.) Tony broke the lock on the door to get it open so I could get a clean, dry diaper to change Vincent. Tony, of course, replaced the lock and fixed the damage to the door right away.

Tony and I were happy in this picture.

Vince had a doctor's appointment one bitter cold winter day when he was about four months old. The person who had told me she would take us to the appointment forgot. I did not drive and our only vehicle was with Tony at work anyway. I decided I would bundle Vince up and put him in the baby coach and walk there. What choice did I have?

I got him outside and it was so cold that he stopped breathing! I was frantic. I didn't know what to do. He was looking blueish and I was so scared. I ran to the older lady who lived downstairs, even though she would never have been my choice to ask for help. She was generally pretty disagreeable, as I have already told you. But

I was desperate. I told her my baby quit breathing. She grabbed Vince, turned on her oven, opened her oven door and held my baby near the open oven. I thought, oh no, this crazy woman is putting my baby in the oven. But he started breathing. It was like a miracle to me. When she found out I was on my way to the doctor, she called her daughter, who came and took us to the doctor. I was so grateful to her and her daughter.

It makes sense that all his time growing up, my son Vince has not liked cold wind on his face.

In June of 1958, our second son, Tony Jr., was born weighing 8 lbs. 2 oz.

After two years on Fuller Street, we wanted to move. My cousin, Tony Palma, his brother and his dad helped us find a new place. (Yes, this is the third Tony in my story.) It was a pretty new, twin-house with a finished basement on Carriage Street in East Philadelphia. My cousin Nick lived close by too. It was like brand new to me! I was so anxious to move there.

We put down a $1,000 deposit on the property that cost $9,000. In the meantime, Wedgewood Federal Credit Union failed and that was where we had our money. We had used Wedgewood because our uncle had recommended it. Our money was gone. The timing could not have been worse.

I called my brother to tell him because he had money in there too. I told him about the deposit we made and how we needed the rest of the down payment or we would lose the house. He loaned me the $1,000 we needed so we could still get it. I was so thankful. We paid my brother back and after a while we both got a small percentage back from the credit union failure. Another lesson learned for me.

The Carriage Street two-story house had a kitchen, dining room, living room, two bedrooms and a bathroom. We had a little front yard and a little bit bigger back yard. Across the street I could look out and see past the waist-high stone wall to the beautiful grounds of a Jewish cemetery. The Mount Sinai Cemetery had huge mausoleums and fancy gravestones made of beautiful marble with fine names in Philadelphia's history. Wanamaker and Gimble were two I still remember. Each month they would put the flower-of-the-month on all the graves. It was like living across from a huge park. I loved the open space of the cemetery in the middle of the city. There was a church and a school down on the corner. I could walk to Mass. I liked that, maybe because that was what it was like at home in Italy.

After our second son was born we needed more space. We moved to a twin-house on Cottage Street. This picture is all the twin-houses in a row on Cottage Street.

While we lived on Cottage Street, an older Italian lady, Elizabeth, would come to visit every morning.

Her daughter would drop her off. She would stay with me all day until Tony came home, then he would take her home. She was really nice and a lot of company for me. She would share cookie and cake recipes with me. We all liked having her around. I had tried to explain to the boys that their Nonnas were across the ocean. They took to calling Elizabeth grandmom, and of course, she loved it. She did feel like family. Her son, Otto, is the godfather for my son Tony. When we were making plans to move out of the city into the suburbs, Elizabeth and her son, Otto, loaned us $2,000.

7-Capitolo Siette

Bristol.

After eight years in our Carriage Street house, we bought a property in December of 1959 and moved to Bristol, a suburb of Philadelphia. The down payment was $1,500 dollars. There was a big two-bedroom apartment upstairs. I cleaned it up and settled my boys in. Downstairs the property had last been a Chevy dealer showroom with a garage for repairs.

The new place was supposed to have a new roof. It didn't. The first big rain, we had a waterfall in the room we were sleeping in.

We were told the showroom was rented out for storage and we would have the rent money from that. We didn't. It turned out that the seller had furniture stored there and he moved it out before we got there. There was NO rent money. We found out later that the shop had a bad reputation. After you brought your car there, it didn't work anymore. Wasn't that great? We had so much to deal with.

One good thing happened. I got pregnant for the third time. My happiness did not last though. I lost the baby, I think it was a little girl, and it made me very sad. After the miscarriage, I just kept bleeding and bleeding. I was in bed for days. Finally, my husband insisted I go to the doctor. I went to the closest hospital, and the doctor told me I was almost at the pearly gates. I didn't know what he was trying to tell me, and asked what gates? I had hemorrhaged and lost so much blood, I almost died. He was talking about the pearly gates of heaven!

After three days in the hospital, I came home. I was moving really slow for a while. I felt great sadness about losing my baby. I was still crying myself to sleep at night. I never had peace; there was worry all the time. It was overwhelming. One night I was so upset that I went upstairs so my son would not see me crying. And I was not happy with his father that night. My husband, Tony, sent little Vince upstairs to get me. He asked me why I was crying and I lied to him and said I had a headache. Vince started crying too and we just cried together for a little bit. He was such a beautiful boy. I hugged him and he told me his dad said to come downstairs. We dried our eyes and went downstairs.

The shop was in pretty bad shape when we bought it. We discovered the wooden walls of the shop were rotten. We replaced them with cement blocks, one wall at a time, as we had the money. A new cement floor was needed, so we did that too. We basically rebuilt the whole place from the ground up. Every extra penny we had was going back into the property. The front of the showroom was all glass, so we changed it to brick with windows above it. We rented the space out to a guy who wanted to put a laundromat there. Before he could do that though, the floor in the showroom had to be reinforced. It was not strong enough for heavy commercial washing machines and dryers. Then that floor needed new tile. Then we had to have some new water piping. Our friend Dominic took care of that. The laundromat was a favorite in our town after a few years. It was a good location. It is still going strong today.

The first year of our body shop business was definitely the hardest. One friend said we would never get out from under the debts. Another person told us he was in debt, but we, we were up to our eyeballs. Businesspeople like Wheat Chevrolet and Dieckhaus Buick were making bets about how long we would last. Dieckhaus said we wouldn't last six months. They were all wrong. Both the Chevy and the Buick dealerships would send Tony work. They liked the job he did, but they would low bid jobs because they knew he needed the work. The owner of Dieckhaus became a big friend of Tony's over the years.

The property had cost us $27,000. That was a lot of money. Tony was a very hard worker and worked two jobs until we got a little ahead. He worked 8 a.m. to 4 p.m., then 5 p.m. to midnight. By the end of the first year the shop was full and busy all the time. He had a tow truck and used that to pick up business. Towing was another way to bring in money, but it required more of Tony's time. He took accident calls from the police and would pick up cars in New York, New Jersey, all over Philadelphia–wherever he could get the job. Sometimes he would be gone all night towing a car. I remember one time he spent the whole night getting a car out of the river. He got a lot of experience working with accidents.

On our way together one day the traffic on the highway was backed up because of a bad accident. Tony walked the long way up to where the accident was and there were two kids stuck in this smashed car, screaming in pain. The emergency services guys were using the jaws of life wrong, wondering why they wouldn't work. Tony showed them the right way to use the tool, and the poor kids were rescued.

Tony was a tool expert, and he was always ready to help people. When he came in under an estimate for fixing a car, he was known to split the difference with the customer. He always said he worked for the customer, not the insurance companies. He got the reputation of not only being good and honest, but he would tackle jobs other people wouldn't. The word spread and he never had to advertise. An example is the time he bought two wrecked Chevy Camaros. One was damaged on the front and the other was damaged on the back. He welded the good, undamaged parts together and our sons had a really nice car. No one could tell it had been two cars. People were really impressed.

Tony was tired all the time, and when he slept, he slept hard. He went to sleep fast and could sleep through anything. When it was time to get up in the morning, I would have to start talking to him trying to wake him. Many days it took some loud hollering to get him up.

When Tony laid down to "take five" (nap), our son, Vince, would lay on top of him and go to sleep too. He was crazy for his father. Vince would cry when his dad left, so Tony would try to sneak out without little Vincent seeing him leave. Tony would go out the big basement window instead of the front door.

It was like Vince knew his dad would be gone for a long time. One of the neighbors asked me if I was beating the kid when his dad was not home. They would hear Vince crying and knew it was when his dad was gone. I told them no, Vince just misses his father.

Tony was coming home after 2 a.m. one morning, after staying late to finish a job before deadline, and just couldn't stay awake the 1½ miles home. He pulled over on the side of the new two-lane highway to rest his eyes. The next thing he knew, there was a cop knocking on his window thinking he was passed out. Tony told him he was just resting a little, but he was fine, just tired. The cop told him he thought that was a good idea for him to rest.

One hot summer day, while at the food store, he fell asleep with his head in the freezer by the ice cream. I couldn't figure out what was taking him so long. I was in the line at the checkout and was getting pretty mad. I went back and there he was, with the door open, the cool air on him, sleeping. He was standing up! Another time, my husband came home after both jobs and sat down to eat. I went on with the things I had to get done. When I came back to the kitchen, he was asleep with his forehead on his coffee cup. The imprint of the cup ring was on his face for two days.

8-Capitolo Otto
Fighting to Survive.

In the property sale contract, it said there was an inspection station in the business, so we thought that would make money for us. That was a lie. As soon as we got in there, the old owner stopped inspections. There was no money coming in for that after all.

The contract also included the installation of an oil/propane tank. When the oil company people came, they said they couldn't fill the tank because it wasn't stable. It rocked back and forth. The feet on the tank were too small for that size tank.

I called the old owner and he came over. He told me, "There was nothing wrong with the tank. You just can't afford to fill it!" We really needed heat for our apartment, for my little boys, so I was very mad at this dishonest man who had lied to us about so many things. I picked up a broken bottle lying on the ground and held it up to him and told him "I won't let Tony kill you, I will kill you myself. I am taking driving lessons too and I will get the car and run over you and keep running over you until you are dead. I will kill you myself and I will go to jail, but I will get out and you will still be dead."

I was so mad! He quickly sent someone over to fix the feet on the tank and didn't show his face around us for a long time. His brother, however, brought his car to Tony to fix. He said he knew his brother, the previous owner, was not right to treat us that way.

I did get my driver's license too, despite the objections of my husband. He told me I'd be sorry if I learned to drive. I ignored him. I practiced in the factory parking lot behind us. Vince, my oldest son, wouldn't come with me in the car when I practiced.

He just stayed outside the fence and watched me drive around and around. Tony was too young to object, so he rode along with me.

I did not get much encouragement from the three men in my life. When I went to the driving test, the man doing the test was a state trooper and he asked me if I was a "war bride." I had no idea what he was talking about. He explained, and I told him no. How funny! I was kind of the opposite of a war bride, as I went back over and got married there after already being in America. When my driving test was done, he said, "Come in and sign the paper, you passed." My husband had driven me to the test and was waiting outside. When I came out, he said, "Don't worry, we can come again. You don't have to pass on your first try." He could not believe I passed; he assumed I wouldn't. He was so surprised, his mouth was open wide.

I don't know why people doubt me. My sons didn't pass on their first time; and they spoke English well. After that, I would help out my husband at the shop by taking the car to pick up an auto part or a check for a repair job for the shop.

One time I had another state trooper follow me the whole way. I was so nervous. I stopped at the place for the check, and he came up to me. I asked him "What did I do? Why are you following me?" He told me I didn't do anything wrong. He asked me if I would sell him the car. I was so relieved. It was a 1956 Chevy, bronze colored, with stripes. It was in good shape. Everyone loved that car. I told him it wasn't for sale, but thanks anyway.

Driving in town one day a big truck in front of me lost a big branch and it fell on my car, leaving a dent. I got the information from the driver–name, driver's license number and license tag. Then I went on to the store. When I got home, I told Tony about it and gave him the information I collected plus my driver's license. He asked why I didn't file a police report, and I told him he knew all the cops down there so he could do it. Tony went to the police station and filed the report. His buddies, seeing my picture on the license, asked Tony, "What is she doing with you?" When he got home, he was so disgusted. He had to tell someone, so he told me what they had said. He was mumbling under his breath about the stupid, no-good guy. I laughed and told him they were just teasing him. He wasn't buying that. Tony was a proud man and that was something he didn't want to joke about.

The area of Bristol we had bought into was so unfriendly. We heard things like, "We don't like people who move into our town," and "You are outsiders." That's what they said to our faces. I could imagine what they said behind our backs. I told them, "Then you should put a fence around your town."

A Greek neighbor was very outspoken, telling me, "The shop is no place to raise kids." I told him, "Buy me a house and I will move." There was definitely prejudice toward us. It was horrible. They made us feel like we didn't count, like we were nobody. We were treated badly because of our name, because we were from another country, because we were Italian. But we were citizens just like them. It was hard to be understood sometimes, and some people didn't even try. This lady across the street had a phone answering service so she knew lots of things about lots of people. She would call me and tell me that my husband was talking to a very attractive woman at the shop, asking me what I thought about that. I just told her he talked to a lot of people at the shop. He was taking care of their cars. She was trying to make me jealous, I guess, but I never had to worry about my husband.

We were learning that in Bristol, everyone is related. Unfortunately for us, this town had other people with our same last name. We were NOT related to them, but people automatically thought we were. The other family had every bill collector in the area after them. They had ruined the reputation of our name, though it was no relation of ours.

When the roof leaked in our apartment, we called every roofer in the phone book. They would hang up when they heard our name. I went to the school to enroll my son, and they said they didn't have any more room for a student with our last name. I said, "Tony let's change our name!" My husband said he was not changing his name for anybody. We sent our boys to the Catholic school.

In our small suburb there were two Catholic churches with schools right across the street from each other. One is the Italian Catholic church and the other is the Irish Catholic church. You know which one we went to, right? I was glad the Italian Catholic parish was named St. Ann's, just like the necklace I had worn since I came to this country. And just like my mother's name, Anna. I hoped St. Ann would help us.

I told my boys that they were going to school to learn. "Listen to what they tell you." This was especially important so that people knew our family was well-behaved and we paid our bills, unlike the other family with the same name. Mother Superior at the school commented to me one day about how well dressed my sons were. I bought all their clothes at Lobel's. It was the best kids' clothes store around. They had pants with a pull string so you could buy a size 2 and then when my son got too tall for a 2, you pulled the string and it would let the hem down and the pants would be the length of a size 3. That way you got more use out of the clothes. They were made well and they lasted. I ironed their shirts and made sure they always looked very nice. The nuns watched everything at the school. That made me happy that other people noticed. I took great pride in how my family dressed. I also wanted to be sure everyone knew we were not the family that didn't pay their bills. When my sons were in the upper grades, a friend of my son's told me, "I wish my mom would look like you." That was nice. I appreciated that. I tried my best.

I did my best to get to know the people who had kids at the school my sons went to. I also wanted to know the kids my sons were friends with at school. I volunteered at school, serving hotdogs on hotdog day, pizza on pizza day and supervising the Friday night dances. I supported the teachers any way I could. When the kids got in trouble they would have to sit in the hall or kneel on beans for punishment. It happened to my son one day. Another mom was there and told me about it. My son did not tell me he got in trouble. I asked him how his day was and he said OK. Then I asked what he did to get put out in the hall. He said, “Why should I tell you; you will just believe the teachers and punish me again.” Well, he was right about that. I supported the teachers. He kept asking me how I knew. He couldn’t figure that out, he thought I had witch powers. The teachers, mostly nuns, had a big job and I wanted them to have my help in that big job. I hoped to fight the prejudice that the other people with our name had created and the prejudice toward Italians that was visible too.

9-Capitolo Nove

Success For The Business.

We had to make a certified check out each month for the mortgage payment and take it to the seller's lawyer. We also had to pay an additional $50 fee to the lawyer each month. Our payments were never late, and we never missed a payment. The guy we bought the place from used to hang around the garage watching what was going on. After he saw how hard we were working and all the improvements we had made, he wanted it back. He said we had not paid; we were behind on payments. But he had just not cashed some of our payments. He thought he could get it back after all our hard work and guessed we would not know what to do, since we could barely speak the language. My husband said it would be ok, don't worry. He said that the old owner was Italian too, so we could trust him. It would work out ok. I wanted to be 100% sure it would be ok. This was something I would have to fight for. It could not go on; it had to stop. I had two kids and they needed a stable, safe life.

First Federal Bank had the first mortgage on the property at 6% interest. The old owner had the second mortgage. I marched into First Federal and asked to see the president. The woman laughed and asked me if I had an appointment. I said no, so I made an appointment and returned the next week. Mr. John Catzin, the bank president, was a very nice man. He listened to my story. He knew the history of the property, as his bank had sold it at a sheriff's sale. That meant the previous owner got it really cheap. He said he didn't know where I came from, but I should have come to him sooner. We had been putting up with this for three years. I told him I wanted 4½% interest. He said the bank's rate they got was 5% so he couldn't go for 5%, let alone 4½%. He told me he would look into things and see what he could do. People from the bank came, took pictures and made assessments of our place. A week and a half after my appointment, Mr. Catzin, called me himself and said, "Come and get your money."

First Federal now had both mortgages rolled into one and we were free of the old owner. I went in and he told me that people couldn't say enough good things about my husband and me. They said we worked all the time, which was very true. So once and for all, we got rid of the horrible man who was taking advantage of us. I will always be grateful to John Catzin. He used to sweep the sidewalk in front of the bank in the mornings. Everyone knew him because he would say hello to people by name as they walked by. What a nice man!

Since we had rented out the old showroom space to a guy for a laundromat, I asked him if I could work for him cleaning the place. He was happy to have me do that. For nine years, I cleaned the laundromat for $35 a week. Every night I cleaned up the messes left by customers. Sometimes I would have to clean it during the day too. That was something I could do to make some money. Tony would get home late at night, when the boys were asleep, and I would go downstairs and clean.

Some of the people who lived around there would send their kids to the laundromat to play during the day. They would make messes and I would have to clean them up. One of the times a machine had overflowed a woman complained to me that the place was always a mess. This was one of the moms who was guilty of sending her kids to play there. I told her, "If you, your sister and your neighbor would keep all your kids at home and not send them here to play, there would be a lot less mess to clean up." I also pointed out that my kids didn't play there.

The money I earned cleaning the laundromat was our food money. I would walk to the A&P grocery store about a mile away and then carry two big sacks home. I would buy two or three chickens. The drumsticks and thighs I would roast with potatoes one meal, and then everything else but the breasts I made into soup for another meal. The breasts I made into "veal cutlets" because Vince came home from school saying there were kids at school who brought veal cutlet sandwiches for lunch. I used to send them to school with fried egg and pepper sandwiches. He wanted to know what veal cutlets were and could we have some of those? I said, "Sure, we can have veal cutlets!" I pounded the breasts out, breaded and fried them up and told the kids they were veal cutlets. I laugh thinking back on this. The kids didn't know the difference.

I wanted my kids to think they had everything their friends had. They didn't want for anything. That was obvious when Vince would tell us about a friend needing or wanting something Vince had. He would just tell them, "You can have it. My mom and dad will buy me more." He was a kind and generous boy. That was a good thing. He didn't know how tight things had been for us.

I enjoyed cooking for my three men. One of the boy's favorites I made by taking sausage out of the casing and frying it while I broke it up into small pieces. I left the oil and added butter, along with rice and cut macaroni (*fideo*), browning it all on the stove top. Then I would add chicken or beef broth or water, depending on what I had. I would cover it and let it simmer until all the liquid was absorbed. The boys called it Italian Rice-A-Roni.

One day Tony was driving us home and he passed a guy sitting on the steps of a house. He said, "I know that guy. That is Alfonse." My husband was the kind of man who thought he pretty much knew everything. I doubted him. What are the odds of driving by a house in Pennsylvania, U.S.A. and seeing someone you knew from back home in the little town of Sant' Agata, Italy? He circled around to take a second look and said, "Yes, that is him." We stopped and sure enough, Tony was right. We didn't even know he had come to the U.S. He used to be on Mount Taburno with Tony when they were young and they watched the sheep, goats and

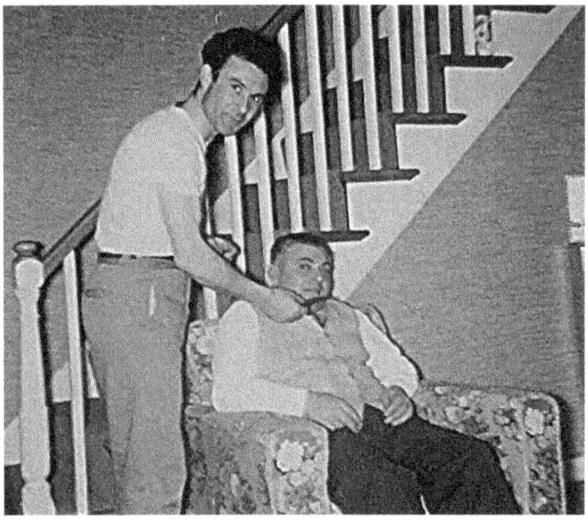

Tony and his friend, Alfonse, from his hometown.

cows. He was a really nice man, a barber. He gave my son Vincent his first haircut.

It is a good memory for me, a friend of my husband's from Italy trimming my handsome son's hair. He told Vince he was a "champion" sitting there looking so grown up in the barber chair. After many conversations with Alfonse, we found out his brother's daughter, Emelia, lived very close to us. We met and hit it off right away. She became my closest friend and the family she had in the states became like my family. Emelia and I celebrated our kids' birthdays together and have been lifelong friends–all thanks to Tony seeing Alfonse on a porch step all those years ago. His sister, Jennie, was a good friend too. I thank God and the Black Madonna for arranging that porch step encounter for me. My prayers about loneliness had been answered.

10 - Capitolo Dieci

Life With My Boys.

Living above a body shop with two small boys was definitely a challenge. I couldn't keep them inside all the time in our apartment. They would look out and see their father working downstairs and wanted to be down there with him. But there were so many dangers lurking for curious young minds exploring their world. I remember telling my husband, "If something happens to these kids, I'll kill you." I love my boys very much and we did our best to make them well-behaved and keep them safe.

I have so many memories of my sons.

When Vince was pretty little, he was playing with another little boy. They got into a fight. Vince bit the other boy. I was mad that Vince bit him and I slapped Vince. The kid he bit was crying. Vince was crying. I was crying. In walks my husband, the funny guy, who looks at all of us and says, "Who died?"

One night at bath time the boys took their clothes off and were heading straight for the tub. I picked up the clothes and one of Vince's sneakers was full of blood. He had stepped on a nail sticking out of some wooden boxes.

Then there was the time the beer truck almost hit Vince on its way to the bar down the street. Vince had been playing in the narrow alley behind the garage that people used as a road, though they weren't supposed to. We stopped that traffic. We used three 2X4's to barricade the alley.

Remember Alfonse? One of his relatives, Jennie's son, Tom, was a lawyer. He helped us out legally on getting the alley behind the shop blocked off. He was a great guy and also solved the problem when a guy was trying to block our property on the front of the

My handsome sons outside the shop.

shop. It was good having someone we could trust, like Tom, through the years when situations like this happened.

Once Vince put his arm in the wringer washer and it was all flat. His dad kept rubbing on it trying to get it back to normal. What a sight that was to see! Then there was the time Tony was trying to give a dog a bone that was in a bag. Little Tony couldn't get it out of the bag quick enough and the dog bit him.

Another day, I found Vince in the bathroom rummaging around in the medicine cabinet. "What are you looking for?" I asked. He said he "just needed a little tape." I said, "What for?" Vince said his brother had a little cut. I went downstairs and Tony's head is bleeding all over the place. Vince had thrown a metal bucket down from the second floor and it hit Tony in the head. Instead of a little tape, Tony got seven stitches.

Tony followed up his stitches with a broken arm. He was riding his new bike. One of the neighborhood kids pushed him and down he went. He had to stay the night in the hospital. My husband and I were so worried about him. We went to the hospital late that night and looked in his window to see him. I had never been away from either of my sons overnight before. We were so sad to be apart from him. I remember thinking that someone might wonder what on earth we were doing out here in the middle of the night looking in his window. We just had to see with our own eyes that he was ok.

The worst thing that happened was when my son Tony was lost. He was with his brother, and they went into the store next door to our property. The next thing we knew, Vince is back, but no Tony. We asked Vince where his brother was and he said he was just here. I was so upset. Just a few weeks before, a little girl had gone missing, and she was found dead down by the river.

A family friend called the police and they, along with the fire department, were searching everywhere. They found Tony on one of my friend's doorsteps crying. He wasn't crying about being lost, though. Someone had given him money for ice cream. Tony had run after the ice cream truck but didn't catch the truck, so he didn't get any ice cream. That is why he was crying.

I fainted when the police came. I thought they had bad news. But Tony was in the car. I grabbed him and ran up the stairs to our apartment. I didn't even thank the police.

An extra special memory of my sons that I have treasured was the time I was upset with Vince. I said to him, "What am I going to do with you?" This handsome little boy of mine looked up at me and said, "Keep me Mom, keep me."

They were good boys and grew into fine men. I am very proud of them.

A family picture from a visit to my brother in Kansas.

11-Capitolo Undici

Moiano.

Many times, I would think about Moiano and what it had been like at home in Italy.

I remember hearing about when my dad came home from his trip to America. I was born while he was gone. I was really little, probably around three years old, when he returned. All the time he was gone, since the day I had been born, I had gotten to sleep with my mom. I loved that. Then here comes this guy I had never seen before, and he was sleeping in my mom's bed instead of me.

I took a broom and tried to sweep him away. I chased him around with the broom hollering at him to get away from my mom. My dad just laughed and laughed. I guess this may have been my first show of toughness – being unafraid to chase a grown man around with a broom.

This is me with a cookie in each hand. This picture was taken and sent to my father in America because I was born while he was gone. I was their first child.

My family had a cow, a donkey, a mule, pigs and chickens. We also had gardens that pretty much grew everything the family would need for the year. We had to be self-sufficient and we pretty much were. It was a lot of work to harvest and preserve everything. For example, we would take the chestnuts out of their prickly covers and put a row of chestnuts in a hole in the dirt. Then we put dirt on them and then another row of chestnuts, repeating the layers until they were all done, and finally topped it all with a layer of sand. The chestnuts would keep all winter long. Then the next year we would do it all over again.

Besides chestnuts, we had pecans, walnuts, pears, peaches, figs, apples, cherries, persimmons, several kinds of grapes (we made our own wine), lots of tomatoes, eggplant, corn (one of my favorites), lettuce, several kinds of peppers, string beans, wheat, onions, squash, garlic, broccoli rabe, carrots and potatoes. Up in the mountains we had olive trees and asparagus that grew wild there.

The kitchen was the center of everything for my family in Moiano. There are many kitchen stories. Like the time a sack of eels was dumped on the kitchen table. They were squirming all over and us kids ran from the kitchen screaming. Whatever crop was being harvested, it was all dumped on the floor in the kitchen. There would be a mound of potatoes leaving dirt all over. I didn't like how dirty they would make the kitchen floor. I was always using my broom to sweep up the dirt and try to keep the room tidy. The whole field of corn would make such a big pile in the corner of the kitchen that we had to hire someone to help us. It was too exhausting without extra help. We would make a lot of corn meal. Every day there was a pot by the stove with beans. We would let them soak and by dinnertime they would be ready to cook.

I never knew my mom's parents. They died young, one week apart, with her father going first. My dad's parents lived with us. I liked that. My grandpa looked out for me. Every Christmas a pig was killed, and I hated the squealing, the smell of blood, the whole thing. I would lock myself in the bathroom until my grandpa would come and tell me it was over and it was safe to come out now.

Maybe he felt sorry for me because I had scarlet fever as a child. My parents were told by the doctor that I had no chance to make it. They had sewed me a burial dress and everything. They said I woke up really hungry. I sure fooled them. My Nonna said it was a miracle. I guess my toughness is a lifelong trait. It helped me when I was young, through my immigration to the U.S., all through my life, and into old age.

My life as a child was pretty simple. I would put a little soap on my finger to clean my teeth and splash water on my face to clean my face. We had no toothbrushes or washcloths. Breakfast was bread pulled into pieces and soaked in milk, or my mom would beat a raw egg with a little milk and have us drink it.

Every five or six days my mom would bake a big, round loaf of bread. My mom was fussy about keeping the bread. She kept it in a basket hoisted up high in the kitchen to keep it away from pests and nibbling children. My brother Giovanni knew how to get some bread though. The bread would get pretty hard toward the end of the loaf so mom would fry it in a pan with olive oil, water, spices, beans, squash, broccoli rabe, or whatever leftovers we had. That was our tasty meal that night.

We all had chores at home. Being the oldest child, I had more chores than the rest of my siblings. I had to do the dishes. My mom would call me ducky because I liked to play in the water when I was doing the dishes. I was drawn to cleaning and rinsing the dishes in the water. Another job I had was to carry this 5-gallon jug (*bitune)* balanced on my head up over the mountains to get milk. People have joked that carrying that heavy weight on my head contributed to my shortness, but I don't know about that. One time my friend cracked her container, and she switched it out and took mine. She lied about it, trying to get me in trouble. When I got home, I told my mom the truth of what had happened and we exchanged it with the company. Honesty was important in my family.

We would wash the clothes by putting soap in a big wooden

tub and then dumping boiled water with ashes in it on top of the clothes. We let them sit overnight. The ashes bleached the clothes. After that we would rinse the laundry in the creek. We used a stone washboard at the creek. It was hard work.

This is me.

After my chores were done, I liked to play hopscotch and play with my rag doll. I used to tie stones to my shoes to make it like high heels and pretend I was a grown-up. Sometimes I would dress up in my mom's clothes and walk around in mom's one pair of real high heels. When I was older, I liked to comb my girlfriend's hair. They liked it when I fixed their hair. That was nice because when I tried to pull my little sister in to comb her hair, she never wanted me to and would run away.

We liked to climb up on this one rock wall and sit there talking and watching what was going on. One time, I got up on the wall and one of my friends asked me to help her get up there. I reached down and she grabbed my hand but instead of her coming up, I got pulled down. I fell and broke my ankle. My friend felt bad, but it was an accident. I went home and my mom beat egg whites and shredded a piece of rope into fine hairs and made a wet pack around my ankle with the rope hair and egg whites. That was my "cast." No hospital or doctor needed, just my mom. That is the way it was done back then.

Another time I was riding my dad's tame donkey. Just when I got in front of my aunt's house someone close by set off some firecrackers. That scared the old donkey, and it threw me off. I broke my wrist. I was scared to ride donkeys or mules after that.

I remember walking a mile and a half to get water at the well with my girlfriend. There was a heavy wood bucket on a pulley that you let down into the well and then you would bring the bucket back up full of water. It was a two-person job at our age and size. We were working on getting the bucket up and a horse got loose and came running up on us at the well, raring up on his back legs over our heads. We were lucky we didn't get pushed in the well or killed. That scared me a lot. After that I just stayed away from donkeys, mules and horses.

As a child I looked forward to September every year for the Feast of the Black Madonna. The *festa* was better than Christmas because the celebration lasted eight days and it was all outdoors in nice weather. Every night there were church services and lots of party time. This was a big social event for our small town, and you got to see everybody. Neighboring towns would also come to each other's *festas*, so there were lots of people in our town. There were sweets for sale, carnival rides, merry go rounds, music, beautiful decorations with thousands of lights up and down the streets, a parade with a statue of our patron saint, the Black Madonna, and a huge fireworks show. This was the only time of the year there were fireworks and for our tiny town they were BIG fireworks. It was a lot of fun.

Festa lights in the streets of Moiano.

When people left Moiano, if they could, they would return for this

The Black Madonna is carried through the streets while people sing and donations to the church are pinned on the statue. My dad always proudly pinned on the American money we sent home every September.

festa. If you couldn't make it, you sent money for the church and it was pinned below the statue of the Black Madonna during the procession around town. My father was proud that my brother and I sent money every September and he would pin it to the statue so all could see the American money. It was a sign to all that though we were in America, we treasured our Italian home.

When I was about 14 or 15, for two hours after school a couple days a week we went to the convent, and the nuns taught us how to embroider. We had to work on our dowry (*coredo*). I embroidered my initials and a decorative edge on 15 to 20 bedsheets, as well as nightgowns, pillowcases and tablecloths. When I went to America, I left my dowry in Italy, and my little sister used it for her wedding. Her initials were the same as mine, M. P. That was good, as she didn't have her own. My sister was not interested in embroidery, sewing and cooking. She was a tomboy and preferred being outside.

12-Capitolo Dodici

The War.

When I was 12, the war came.

The courtyard that was created by four houses together was where I would play with other children while the mothers were working and talking. I especially liked watching one woman. She was one of the oldest and she was always weaving baskets. I wanted to learn how to do that too. One day, the basket lady was joined by more women who started gathering, and more and more arrived. They started crying and praying. They were all so upset but no one wanted to tell us kids what was happening. We thought someone had died.

Then one by one, the women started to go away. After most of them were gone, the basket lady told us the war had come. The men in our town would have to go to war as soldiers. We had heard war stories. Even as kids we knew this was bad. Almost everyone had a son to be called up in the army. That's why the women of Moiano were so upset.

The war changed our lives. Before the war, the worst thing that had happened was an occasional mild earthquake that made us sleep outside and away from the heavy stone and marble of our homes. Now there were bombs falling right close to us. A cannon ball landed in our cemetery and unearthed buried people. The planes would come every night, and we had to sit in the dark.

There were no jobs and no food. Mussolini took everything. He took all our wheat and corn, except for a tiny amount. For more than two years we had no sugar, and we couldn't get any. To get flour we had to hide some wheat, then go over the mountain with a donkey and make flour at night. We just couldn't get caught.

Mussolini also took all the copper and pans. He left only one pan to cook with. He took everyone's wedding rings too; everything gold.

There was only one good thing about Mussolini. I liked that he had the girls march. Before, only the boys got to go. I had to stay home and help my mother. My mom wanted to take on Mussolini! She didn't want me to go, even though Mussolini ordered it. The parish priest told my mom she had to let me go. Every Saturday the boys and the girls would march up and down the streets of Moiano.

The first wave of American soldiers to arrive were men that had been let out of prison to fight. My dad taught us that was what the black band on the uniform arm meant. We kept far away from all soldiers, but especially those men with prison armbands. When they came through our town, they were causing many problems. I remember the German soldiers bothering the girls and women, but the American soldiers were worse. That is why I was so scared when my friend and I were followed as we went to get water one time. These two American soldiers followed us all the way to get the water and then all the way back home. As we got close to home, I started calling out to dad. My father took his American passport and showed it to them, warning them to behave as he was an American just like them. He told them he could make a lot of trouble for them by filing a report to command. "Never let me see you again around here," he said. One of the men grabbed my father's passport, looked at it, then kissed it. He told my dad he hoped he would live to return to America.

One American soldier did something to one of my young female cousins. Her father hit the soldier with a hoe and he died. He would not make it home to America.

I was in the mountains walking around and picking up wood with my dad when I saw a black soldier. I stopped. I froze. I couldn't move. I had never seen a black person before, only my

Black Madonna statue. My dad said "Come on, walk. They are not going to bite."

When we knew there were going to be soldiers, German or American, going through town, my sister and I were hidden up in the attic so no harm would come to us. I remember sometimes staying two days in the attic at a time. We hid from them all. They were all pretty scary to me. Towards the end when the Americans were coming to liberate our town, the Germans were scared and were trying to get out of there as fast as they could. It had been raining for days, and their trucks were stuck in the mud. The Germans were going through town gathering up all the boys and men they could find to help push them out of the mud. When the Germans had done this in the past, some of these men were never seen again. My brother, Giovanni, was out on the street when they came through and a German soldier chased him. He ran as fast as he could until he came across a woman in our town we knew well. Rosa Micarole grabbed him and hid him in her hay, so he was not taken away. She saved his life. She had a son two years younger than my brother. People in Moiano took care of each other. We were all grateful to her.

When the war was over, the American troops were cheered as they drove through our town. We would throw bunches of grapes to the soldiers as they waved at us, and they threw us candy and chewing gum. Watching the parade of soldiers, my Nonna saw the black soldiers. She thought the sun had made the people change color. That was the first time she had seen black people in person. My dad told her, "That's not from the sun, they are black." He was proud of his English and asked the soldiers "What took you so long?" One soldier answered, "Well Pop, we had a little trouble."

Some of our cousins who lived in New Jersey, one of their sons, was in this group of soldiers. He looked my dad up and stayed with us a week. We all enjoyed that. It was fascinating watching him talk to Dad. My dad especially had a good time as he rarely got a chance to show off his English.

I had relatives in America fighting against Germany. I had relatives in Italy fighting for Germany. I found out later that there were Italians in prison camps in the U.S. during the war. There were Italians in German prison camps too. My husband's brother was a prisoner of war for seven years. What a mess! Americans have no idea how lucky they are to have lived without war in their country.

13 - Capitolo Tredici

The House With Grass All Around It.

In Moiano the town was so small, everyone knows everyone's business. That was one thing I did not like about home. Some of the things I liked I brought with me.

In Moiano we had two kitchens–one out front and one in the back. I liked that. I wanted two kitchens in my American house. Our goal was to build our own house.

This is my beautiful home with grass all around it. That is what my son asked for.

Looking out the apartment window one day, my son said he wished we had a house with grass all around it like the house across the street from the shop. Business had been good; the word had spread that our place did good work. In 1966 it was no trouble to get a mortgage for our house and property purchase. We had proven ourselves in our adopted town. The bank officer asked what we had done to the people in Bristol. No one could say a bad word about us. What a change from earlier days! Persistence had paid off.

We bought a double lot just a few minutes from the shop. The neighborhood was a good one. The foot doctor, the eye doctor and the family doctor lived across the street from our lots. Our lots looked like a forest, overgrown with trees and weeds. You could not see any ground. There was lots of trash too, because people had been dumping stuff there for years. A year later we also bought a second double lot behind what we already had. Two brothers had these lots with plans to build, but one got transferred and one of them died. We were happy to have so much space of our own. We had one home on the property that normally would have four houses on it.

We got the lots cleared out but it took a long time. A good friend of ours, Tony DiMaio (Tony number four in this story) was a big help, pulling down the trees and brush. Back then you could burn this kind of stuff and that is what they did. They saved the trees that were in good shape and in a good place.

I would take food and drinks to everyone working on our building site. I had to just drop it off and leave. That was after my first of many encounters with poison ivy. I was covered with it. The others had no problem with the ivy. And that's good.

This Tony was easy going and whenever things were not going the way he wanted them to, he would say, "What are you going to do?" My husband started saying that after he heard his friend Tony say it so much. Before long, I too was saying, "What are you going to do?" The older I got, the more I seemed to say that.

My husband, Tony, knew Carmine, the owner of the plumber's supply shop in town. He brought his cars to Tony to fix, and Tony bought supplies from him. This guy had built a house and was bragging to Tony about his new home. Tony asked him who built it and was told it was a private contractor. That is just what we needed. We went to see Carmine's new house. It was nice and we liked what we saw. We hired the same builder to build our house. He had a small business like us, and we liked that too. We didn't feel comfortable with some big building company.

I told the builder, "Whatever you do, make sure my basement doesn't have water because I will come find you if it does." He asked me, "How will you find me, I haven't given you my address?" I told him, "I will find you; your name is on the contract." Only once, just recently, when a drain was clogged, have we ever had water in our basement.

The builder made the changes to the plans that we wanted. We made the window in the front bigger, with five sections, and added stone to the front of the house. Tony used to say he added steps to the house so he could always have a place to tie his shoes. He added a step wherever he could, including in the bathroom and office in the basement, and in the kitchen in the basement. Years later, we turned the garage into an office and laundry room–with a step, of course. Then we added a garage that was separate from the house. The insurance was a lot lower if the garage was separate.

This is the view looking out my big window from my living room on the front of my house. I really liked that lamp.

We had a hard time finding anyone to do the stonework to match the original house. We looked and looked and finally found this really old Polish man who was good with the stone. He made the second part exactly like the first part. He did a beautiful job. You would never know that the section with the garage was added later. I cooked his favorite Polish sausage for him when he was working. He was happy working at our house.

Tony's purchasing philosophy was "buy only the best." He was very careful and never bought from anyone who was shady. He always had to have a receipt. He was honorable and did not want any trouble. There were lots of mafia stories, and he wanted no part of scandal of any kind. I am proud of him for that. I thought the same way. That is what we did when building our home. The builder mentioned a few times that we could save some money if we used one thing or another, but Tony always said no. Only the best. Only with a receipt.

Carmine's wife had a sewing machine. I had never had one of my own. Tony bought me a sewing machine. Of course, it was a top-of-the-line Italian model, a Necchi. She and I took sewing lessons together. We each made two dresses. What an improved skill level I had from sewing at the shoe factory and to sewing the edges of cotton to make diapers when I was young, to sewing dresses now. I still have my Necchi machine, but it needs repair and you cannot get the parts anymore. I have a Singer sewing machine, but it is not working very well, and it really frustrates me learning this new machine. As I get older, I'm getting shorter and shorter, and I need a machine that works so I can shorten my pants.

Tony was good about buying the best and latest appliances and gadgets for our home. But the new water-saving washing machine frustrated me. It saved so much water the clothes didn't get washed and rinsed well. I would put the clothes in then manually add a bucket of water on top of the clothes. Then when I turned the machine on, the clothes would weigh more because of that extra water. The machine would use more water in the wash and rinse cycles to give me the clean clothes I wanted. My grandson asked me about this, and I told him what I was doing. He said "Grandmom, you are tricking the machine by outsmarting the sensors." I guess I was!

Over the years we had taken over the laundromat business, so I knew more than the average person about how to wash clothes. I had lots of experience, and I cleaned the clothes Tony and the boys wore at the shop–their greasy, heavily soiled items. I had so much laundry back then that the older lady next door thought I was taking in laundry for money.

Since only the best went into our home, it really is a beautiful home that I am proud of. It has a lot of extras that other houses did not. With an extra deep basement, an outside exit from the basement and even a Nutone whole house intercom system to communicate or play music in every room in the house. That was a big thing back then. On the outside you could see the quality and beauty of our home. A couple of years ago a young boy on a bike was riding past my house. I was out in the front yard, and he stopped when he saw me. He said "Lady, you have the prettiest house on the block." I smiled and thanked him. I had never compared the houses before but once I thought about it, I agreed. It was wonderful giving my sons a place to live away from the business with "grass all around it."

I have a nice big kitchen in my dry basement with a commercial exhaust fan. If you fry peppers as much as I have done, you really benefit from the commercial fan. The whole house doesn't smell like what you are cooking–garlic, onions and those kinds of things. That is where I have done most of my cooking. I have everything just the way I want it, as long as nobody comes in and messes things up. With a good size freezer, plus a second refrigerator, I have lots of space for storing what I make. There is a closet where I put my marinara sauce that I would can myself using tomatoes from my

Frying peppers under the commercial exhaust fan in my downstairs kitchen.

The view out back of my house from my sink in my upstairs kitchen.

own garden. I also canned tomatoes, fried peppers in olive oil, pickled eggplant, pickled green tomatoes and beans, all from my garden in the back yard.

This is the kitchen where I would make homemade *cavatelli* noodles–a family favorite for special occasions. I have my huge wooden board that I have had since I worked at the restaurant in Schenectady, New York, all those years ago. I still use it for *zeppole*, which is kind of like an Italian donut made with potatoes. My granddaughter has already asked for my big wooden board after I am gone. It will bring her good memories of me, I think.

Making breakfast in my upstairs kitchen. I always use two hands.

My frying pans are hung from the ceiling on one side of the kitchen. There are thirteen pans, each with their own special job in my kitchen downstairs and four more in my kitchen upstairs. All my pans–they are true luxury to me. Having the right pan makes the job easier and the food better.

I'd go up and down the stairs a lot of times during the day. So many times, in fact, that my husband fixed the door to the basement so I didn't have to turn the doorknob to come up from downstairs. I would just push it, and it opened easy. That was a big help, as most of the time my hands were full. Many, many happy hours have I spent in my kitchens. Most of my life, really.

All my downstairs pans have a special purpose. Some people collect shoes, I collect pans. These are just the ones I have hanging up.

14 – Capitolo Quattordici

No Job Too Big Or Too Small.

We worked so hard, I'm not sure how we had the strength to do it all.

The auto body shop was busy. Tony had worked at a body shop and was knowledgeable and good at it. He developed a loyal following. Many customers would wait to have their cars done until Tony had time for them.

We were a mom-and-pop kind of place. We did the paperwork, billing and estimates. I would help Tony with whatever I could. I was the auto body secretary. Tony would paperclip the envelopes of all the bills we'd received into a bundle. I would look at the return address and write it on our envelope to mail the check out in. I hated doing that, but I did it. Ever since people had made fun of my writing, I was self-conscious about it. It took me a long time.

Having your own business is an expensive undertaking. Tony had two or three guys employed at a time to help with the bodywork. We had to offer them health insurance. Our small group plan was high dollar, and to have maternity benefits for their wives, we had to pay maternity benefits for me. I was well past the age of needing that benefit. Funny though, I never had it when I needed it.

Tony taught the guys who worked for him a lot. He was a perfectionist, making them redo things if they didn't meet his standard of perfect or if they didn't do it the way he told them to. He trained his guys so well that any guy who moved on from Tony's shop could get a job fast, once they heard where he had worked before.

Tony had the best reputation in the area. His motto, "No Job Too Big Or Too Small" was printed on his Valley Auto Body business cards. They could have said, "No One Will Do It Better" too! One of the insurance men told us our garage was the cleanest one in the whole state. Tony kept it that way, and he made sure the guys working there did too.

The guys that worked for us were treated well, like family. I mean really nice, like I treat family, not the way some of my family had treated me and my brother. We showed them respect and they were always respectful to me. I would bake them birthday cakes and invite them for dinner. One of them told me years later that I always treated them like I was their mom. One of the guys, Frank, worked for us for many years. Maybe it was that people saw how we treated him or because he was Italian too, customers often thought he was our son. That made me smile.

We had some really good guys work at our shop. Many stayed in touch. Felipe, who used to work at the shop, I still get to see. He lives down the street from me and cuts my grass. My husband never called him Felipe, he called him Phil. Not sure why, maybe because there were no Felipes in Italy. The last time Phil was here he gave me a big hug.

Another guy, Howard, called a few years back to say goodbye. He was not expected to live much longer, and he wanted to talk to us one more time. He wanted me to forgive him for all the trouble he gave me. He said if he survived, he would come see us again. He died that next week. We were happy to hear from him. He didn't give me that much trouble.

Our workers had respect for us. They used to call me when Tony was out picking up a car and closing time came around. I didn't know Tony wasn't there. He did not tell anyone where he was going or how long he would be gone. He was the boss, you know. He didn't answer to anyone. His plumber friend, Dominic, told me if my husband was not careful, something was going to happen to him. Sometimes when he went to pick up a car after a wreck, the cops had already left, and he had some close calls with angry people who did not want him to tow their car. It was dangerous and I worried about Tony. We worried about Dominic too. He died when he was electrocuted on a plumbing job while putting in a sump pump for a customer. We were sad to lose him. He was a good friend.

There was danger everywhere, that was for sure. The guys at the shop sympathized with me and were very kind to me. They understood what my Tony was like. They would lock the place up and go home. At least when they called, I knew Tony wouldn't be coming home for a while. I never knew when he would appear for dinner. It drove me crazy. But I knew there was no changing this stubborn but hard-working man I married. Tony was serious about building a business that he could pass down to his sons one day. That was how it was done in Italy. Tony continued making our name a good one in this town. Reputation was important and he really cared about his customers.

One customer needed his car done for his wedding and we nearly killed ourselves to make that happen. I remember Tony working all night to finish the bodywork. Then I cleaned it up inside after I finished cleaning the laundromat that night. We got it done at 6:30 a.m. the day it had been promised.

There were some customers who took advantage of us. I know there were people who said they would pay, even pay extra for a rush job, and Tony would work day and night to get it done but NOBODY paid. One I clearly remember was a wealthy family in town and it was their teenager's pickup truck. The mom and the kid promised to pay. Tony was out at least $1,500, just for parts. That was really a lot of money back then. With the labor, it was a big bill, and they could afford to pay. But they didn't. There were far too many customers who skipped out on their bills.

Most customers were good, though, and became friends for life.

One lady who had wrecked her car and scratched up her face was crying really hard and wringing her hands. I comforted her and brought her a cup of coffee. I talked to her until she calmed down. I know it is upsetting when you have an accident. I felt bad for her. From that day on, every Christmas we would hear from her. She appreciated the kindness and became our lifelong friend.

Another customer, a kid in town, had taken his father's Cadillac out without permission while his father was out of town. He had an accident. He and his mother came to us, begging Tony to get it done before the dad returned. Remember the lady earlier in my story who told me they didn't like people from other places? This was her sister, the lady who let her kids play in the laundromat and make it a mess. This is the same lady years later and this was one of those kids who used to mess the laundromat up. She said she would pay for the repairs if her son didn't. You know what? The Cadillac was ready before the father returned. The boy couldn't afford to pay all at once so he would pay as much as he could each month until the full balance was paid off. It took years. Later on, this kid worked for one of the phone companies and sold portable phones. Tony was one of *his* customers! Year after year, he would not let Tony pay for his phone. I asked him once, "How long are you going to keep paying for that Cadillac?" He answered that he wouldn't be alive without Tony fixing that car for him, because his dad would have killed him. So, he would keep giving Tony free phones.

People remember when you treat them right and do a good job. We were very proud everyone in town now respected our last name. We had turned things around from when we first came to Bristol.

At one point, Tony had hurt his back and an adjuster from Prudential noticed Tony was not feeling good. He offered Tony a job at Prudential on the spot. Tony wanted to know what he would be doing. "Writing estimates," the Prudential adjuster said, "just like you do now." Tony told me he didn't think he could do it because of all the time he took to research the right English words and spellings for the estimates. That was what he had to do, and it was really hard for him. He was a proud man and didn't ask for help. He never asked for help on driving directions either. In his checkbook he kept a handwritten list of how to spell all the combinations of amounts that could come up to be written on checks. Spelling in your second language is hard, and he wanted to do it right.

He was unsure of how to do credit cards at restaurants with tips and everything, so rather than be embarrassed about not knowing, he would just carry a lot of cash with him. He caught on fast after he found out, but that shows the dignity and pride he displayed in every part of his life. I was proud of these traits. I was glad he was that kind of role model for my sons. I wanted them to appreciate and value their father and me for all we have achieved in our adopted country. The things that my sons take for granted by being born in this country, my husband and I struggled with. We wanted our boys to have a better life than us, and we made sure they did. Our priority was always our sons.

The boys got many benefits from their dad having a body shop. The business paid for private college for them both. They got to pick where they wanted to go, and when they graduated, they had no student loans to repay. They had a credit card for gas and emergencies that we paid the bills on. They would come home and I would do their laundry for them while they studied. Another benefit was they always had the nicest car around. Other kids admired my sons' cars and were jealous. Their Chevy Camaro sportscar was the champion of their high school. My husband made that car happen. Without him getting it cheap because it needed repair, we never could have afforded that car for the boys. When they were away at college, they always had safe and stylish cars to drive back and forth. I also made sure they left with a trunk full of food for them and all their friends.

Once a state trooper stopped my son and he looked in the trunk. There was a big pot of sauce, *pizza piene*, Easter bread, cookies, etc. and the trooper asked them where they were coming from. A bakery? He thought it looked good and wanted some himself. Guess that was quite a surprise from what he thought was in their trunk.

15 - Capitolo Quindici

Changes And Losses.

My sister had wanted to come to America. I did all the paperwork for her and then she decided she'd rather stay in Italy. I would have liked having her here with me. On one of my trips home, Dad told me, "Maddalena said Maria went to America and America came here to me." I think she meant that I went to America for opportunity, and she benefitted from the opportunities in Italy improving over the years.

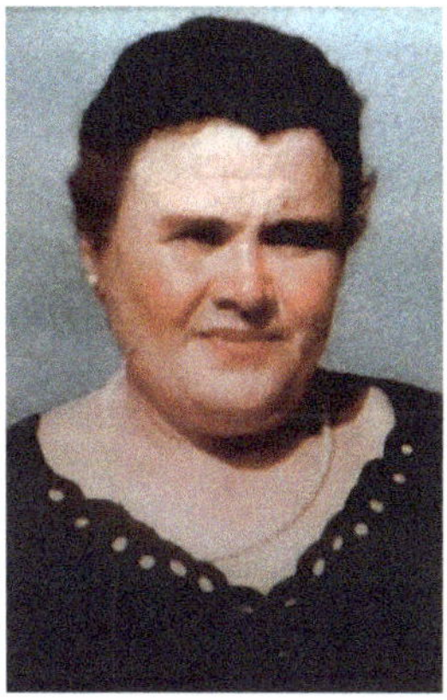

My beautiful sister, Maddalena.

She made her choice. She had no regrets about staying in Italy. She married and had two sons, just like I did. My brother Roberto also stayed in Italy, married and had two sons. They all did well in Italy. Because my brother John and I left, all the property in Italy was split in two instead of four. They got not only their share, but ours too. That was good for them and helped them do well.

I kept up with what was going on with my family in Italy by talking to friends who called back home to Italy a lot. My friend Liberata, who lived in New Jersey, made weekly calls to Moiano and then would call me to catch me up on the latest. Liberata and her husband Giovanni talked Italian all the time. It was funny, because my sons would know when Liberata had called because I would be talking to my sons in Italian when they got home from school. They'd say, "Oh, you talked to Liberata today." Smart

An original drawing of my family by artist Ray Craighead, a gift from my niece Giuliana. We had no picture of all of us together.

kids.

I was glad to have visited my hometown three times since my wedding. My husband did not want to go back. He was such a stubborn man. The first two times, I went without him. It was embarrassing for me to go without him. But I always did the right thing and visited his family. I got very tired of hearing his mom and family complain about how they wished they could see him. I would apologize. But they knew. I had tried to get him to come.

I went with my brother the first time. Then I went with my brother and my younger son, Tony. My brother took his entire family another time and videotaped a message for my husband from his mom. She was a small lady, but her voice was very big as she scolded him in Italian for not coming to see her. When my sons saw this video of their grandmom in Italy, one of them said, "No wonder dad left." You did not need to know any Italian to understand Tony was in big trouble with his mom!

That did the trick, and the last time I went, my husband did go along with my brother and his wife. That was the last time I saw my dad. He was not well. He was in and out of it and did not recognize anyone. In the middle of the night, he called for a drink of water. I went to him with a glass of water. He took the glass and said to me "They told me you were coming." He knew it was me! In the morning, he didn't know me again, but I was so glad I was there to have that last brief moment in the middle of the night with my father. My father passed away in 1993 at 97 years old.

It was so funny how when I would get ready to leave Italy, people in the town would come to me with packages for their relatives in America. One would say, "Take this to my sister," and she lived in California. Another person's family member was in Florida. The hometown people had no idea of just how big America was. I had to explain to them that I had never been to California or Florida because they were far away from me. I could not deliver their packages.

The year 2001 was a bad one. My husband and I never celebrated our wedding anniversary. In Italy it just wasn't done, it was just another day. But on our 49th anniversary, 9/11/2001, we were horrified by the terrorist attacks. Since we lived in the Northeast, the attacks were very close. As Americans, we felt such outrage and sadness for the loss of lives. My brother and his wife were visiting our parents in Italy at the time. That was scary, not knowing if they would be able to safely return, with all the planes grounded and the hatred abroad for Americans. But they made it home.

Tony and I having coffee after a dinner out.

Not long afterwards, one of my brother's nephews, who lived through the attack in New York City, came to stay with us for a long weekend. He said it was so good to get out of the city. Upon his arrival, he promptly fell asleep in our family room. In an uncomfortable looking position, amid lots of noise and commotion, he slept for the longest time. When he finally woke up, he said he hadn't slept that good since the attacks. I feel so bad for all the loss caused on 9/11.

A month later, we were feeling another personal loss. My little sister lost her battle with breast cancer. That made me very sad. I missed out on so much time with her. She was only fourteen years old when I left for America. I have her memorial card framed on my shelf in my family room. Thoughts of her are always with me.

My mom had died in 1985 after an especially bad bout of pneumonia. I have heard people say pneumonia is an old person's friend. I wonder if my mom felt that way. My father would still write me letters after my mom died. He was losing friends and relatives at a pretty fast pace. He would write that he was alone. No one his age was left. I now see what he meant about being left after others are gone. The same thing has happened to me. But I am lucky to still have two brothers, one in Italy and one in America.

My American brother John visiting me after he too was widowed.

I will always feel closest to my brother who came over with me. We have shared so much. With the moves Tony and I made, we didn't have the opportunity to develop long term friendships like we would have if we were in Italy. There, the kids you went to school with knew you all your life. But no matter where I moved, my brother John was a comfort to me.

My dad told us both that he wished we lived closer. So did I. We had a better life coming

John and I have a good time together.

here, but for me it was lonelier than if I had stayed in Italy. My brother lives in Kansas and I am in Pennsylvania, where our father began his American dream for us. My brother was lucky to live very close to his wife's family. I was happy for him. That gives you a sense of security with family close. His kids had grandparents, aunts, uncles and lots of cousins, because he married a girl in America. For our kids, with both parents from Italy, they had very few relatives here, and my brother's family was over a thousand miles away.

I can thank the U.S. Air Force for my brother settling down so far away. He was stationed in Kansas and that's where he met the smart and pretty American girl who became his wife and my American sister-in-law. I will always be grateful to my sister-in-law Rosemary, because I am happy to have her six kids, nine grandkids and two great grandchildren in my life to love.

I have eight nephews and only two nieces. My nieces are pictured with me here, when they took me on a mini vacation.

Even my sister-in-law's sister, Margaret, her kids and grandkids call me Aunt Maria! That gives me seven more kids and 18 grandkids and six great grandkids to love in my "family" in America.

16-Capitolo Sedici

Not So Golden.

In my eighties, I started having bloodwork that was not in range. My platelet count was climbing higher and higher. My family doctor sent me to an oncologist. That was scary because even I knew that meant cancer. My younger sister dying with breast cancer was in my mind too.

After more tests I was diagnosed with essential thrombocythemia (ET), a rare, chronic blood cancer in which a person's bone marrow makes too many platelets. No one I knew had ever heard of ET. I was told it only happens to 1 in 100,000 people. No one knows how you get it either.

I was lucky to see Dr. Farzana Sayani, who had treated this before. She sat down with me and explained this unknown cancer. I thought it was the end, but she told me this was a cancer you live with. It was like she gave me back my life. When I walked out of her office, I was so grateful for her care. She is a wonderful doctor.

I was put on chemotherapy drugs that are so toxic I have to wear rubber gloves to handle the pill. It seems really odd, because I have to swallow this pill and there are no rubber gloves inside. The side effects of the chemo drug are bad and many times I have had to stop for a while. I worry my platelet count will go real high when I am off the medicine. There are daily headaches; some days are definitely worse than others. The bottoms of my feet get fiery red and are so sore I cannot walk on them. When I get these bad reactions, I go off the medicine for a while and then start back up when the symptoms are gone.

I don't want to slow down but with this disease I have no choice. It slows me down. I just cannot do what I used to do. It is hard because no one can see that you are sick. They cannot see how bad you feel. I am tired of people telling me, "Well, you look fine!" Looks can be deceiving and I am not one to complain, but I sure do not feel fine. Some days I feel ok and some days the headache is unbearable and my brain is in such a fog I cannot concentrate or think clearly. That is frustrating, especially since I want to get things done. We will see what happens next. I am a big stroke risk with this. That is my worst fear, to be helpless after a stroke and have to rely on caregivers for the rest of my days. Or it may progress to leukemia, which means it is time for palliative care only at that point. The only sure thing is there is no cure.

My husband was not in good shape either. He was famous for not going to the doctor and if we managed to get him to go, he wouldn't do anything the doctor said to do. So much so, that we took to calling him "doctor."

It is not surprising then that he put off heart surgery until they had to transport him by ambulance between hospitals for emergency surgery. They knew if they let him go home, we would never get him to the other hospital for surgery. He was that surgeon's oldest patient to get bypass surgery. After surgery, he didn't want to wake up. The surgeon said, "Everything went ok, but we don't know if he had a stroke while we were working on him." Hearing that and seeing how bad he looked, I nearly fainted. The surgeon grabbed my hand and said "Hey, I don't want to have to work on you too." Luckily, he came through it ok. Many other health issues have arisen since then for him.

Even though I don't feel well myself, I am taking care of him. I helped him with the cleaning and bandaging on his legs when he had an infection. The infection got so bad that I had to call 911 for an ambulance. Tony was so mad at me, but it was the right thing to do. When he was released that time from the hospital, I remember Tony telling the doctor he didn't need anyone to come by the house to change the dressing, because I "wanted to do it." He just didn't want anyone else in the house. The home health people were probably glad though. Tony was a tough patient to deal with. I know that so well. I did my best for him, helping him bathe and dress and take his medicines. I asked him what he wanted to eat and would make anything he asked for, and even if then he wanted something else, I would make it too. I was watching him get thinner and thinner. He was having so many problems and just could not eat. I tried everything. I remembered his family in Italy and knew that his mother and brother had something wrong toward the end of their lives. They quit eating too. I was so worried about him. Some days, with my headaches, leg cramps and the lack of energy, it was just too much. It was so hard. I looked around and saw all the things that needed to be done and it upset me. I didn't like it. But I had no choice. I just can't do what I used to do. And what I still do takes me so much longer than it used to. It is so frustrating for me.

This is not the way I thought my later years would be spent. When we were young, working so hard, my husband promised me we would travel when he retired. The only traveling we do is back and forth to the doctors and the pharmacy and the hospital. People talk about the "Golden Years." Well, it doesn't feel golden.

When my mom got mad at me, she would tell me I was just like my grandmother, Maria Michela. When Nonna was mad, she would tell my mom, her daughter-in-law, that she was not going to live there anymore. She would go upstairs to her room that she shared with me and my brother and then send me downstairs when she needed something. She would tell me to go cut some *prosciutto* and bread and bring it up to her. I would always do what Nonna said. She stuck up for us kids. When my mom was mad at us and threatened to hit us, Nonna would tell my mom she was going to call the cops.

Nonna planted jalapeno peppers in the garden every year. She would dry them on a string, then in the winter when she wanted some, she would soak them in water and fry them. One time all of us kids were crying from the pepper in the air when my dad came in. He told his mom, "If you want to kill yourself with those peppers, go ahead, but don't kill my children."

My dear Nonna, Maria Michela, shared by Cousin Mira.

She was a character and a great storyteller. She would appreciate me telling these stories.

One of the favorite stories I heard about her was about the time after I had gone to America and my family got an electric light in the kitchen. My Nonna wanted it off, so she hit it with a broom. It was off all right! It made a big pop and broke into lots of pieces on the floor.

She had a lot of wisdom and shared sayings with us like, "Two parents can take care of ten kids, but ten kids can't take care of two parents." She used to say, "You have to eat a ton of salt with a person to really know a person."

Well, after 66 years of feeding my husband, it has been a ton of salt. I definitely know him. Nonna was right. That saying would have worked with ice cream too, because when he was feeling good, the last thing he ate every night was ice cream on top of a piece of cake.

Nonna also said the angel of death didn't want to get the people and take them to death. So, he asked God to give them some sickness so it wouldn't be so hard to take people to death. She would say, "No one gets out of here alive." She was always telling us to eat (*mange*) saying it's the only thing you take with you. I didn't understand then. But I sure do now.

Maria Michela lived to 100 years old. I keep a picture of her in my house. I loved her so much.

17-Capitolo Diciassette

Losing My Husband.

The year I turned 90 brought many changes for me. Just like the rest of my life, I was not in control of the new challenges I faced. My husband, Tony, passed away after our 66 years together.

He was a stubborn man with a hard head (*testa dura*–proper Italian) and *(copa doste*–dialect in Moiano), but he was a good man. He worked hard. He was a faithful man, a good father and good provider. He had kept his promises to me, except for the one about traveling after retirement.

The day before he died, I was getting ready to leave the hospital with my sons and he was telling me something. I leaned close trying to hear better what he was saying, but I could not make it out. I wasn't even sure if it was Italian or English at that point. He was upset that I didn't understand.

At home I kept trying but could not figure out what he was trying to tell me. The next day I took a pad of paper and pen so he could write what he was trying to say. But that next day he was too weak to even try to talk or write. That was the day he left me forever.

No matter how trying a husband is, when you are losing him and facing the rest of your life alone, you feel a huge loss. It is so hard. Many days later I figured out his final message to me. He was telling me he loved me. He had never said that before, so no wonder I could not guess what he was saying. I knew he loved me, but he was never the type of person to say that to me. The only person I had ever heard him tell he loved them was my niece when he was talking to her on the phone. He would say it in a sing-song way, like he was almost joking around, but he said it to her multiple times. He was not comfortable saying it seriously. I had never heard him say it to me or the boys. My niece did not know until after he was gone that she was the only one he expressed his love to out loud. I know it touched her heart.

My husband thought that he was going to live forever. He told me that I shouldn't worry about money because if we needed more money, he would just work more hours. I tried to explain to him that he would not be physically able to work an auto body job all his life. Our bodies get old and he would not be 36 years old forever. But "no worry about a thing" was what he would always tell me.

He could live that way, but I could not. I got some great advice from my older and wiser friend Jennie. She was the sister of the guy on the step spotted by my husband as we drove down his street, remember? She told me to put money in the bank every chance I got. I thought that was a great idea. She explained to me how to get savings bonds and CDs. I didn't know how to do that. She gave me the instructions and the confidence to do this.

Jennie told me I could never save too much. I valued her advice and that is exactly what I did. My husband would give me a couple hundred dollars to go buy something I needed or wanted, and I would put it in the bank. When he found out he got mad. He gave me a credit card and told me to charge everything. He wanted me to spend the money, but every time I could, I put money in the bank. Having savings eased my mind. That feeling of security was most important to me.

My friend Jennie and me.

When my friend, Emelia, and I would go shopping I would ask

My friend Emelia and me at my 90th birthday party. Photo thanks to Betty.

her advice on which blouse did she like better on me. She would tell me to buy them both. I just couldn't do that.

Emelia was great company all my days. We talked on the phone frequently. Many times, we would plan our doctor appointments together, and since Emelia didn't drive, I drove her. After the doctor, we would shop and eat lunch. There were short trips organized by the senior citizens in the area that we would go on together. One of my favorites was to the Longaberger Basket Factory. I made a beautiful basket with my own hands. It was fascinating to me and brought back memories from my childhood of the basket lady.

Emelia and I were like sisters. Photo thanks to Ann Marie, who is my godchild.

I kept adding to our savings, and this time I made sure that whatever I put in the bank was FULLY insured so I would not lose any money like before. I knew what that was like and I knew what it was like feeling trapped because of not having enough money. I wanted to be sure that neither of those things happened to me again. When I reached the insurance limit of bank number one, I would go to bank number two, then three.

When your husband is not worried at all, it makes you worry more. Saving was even more important for me to do because when you have your own business like we did, there is no pension. It was all up to me. As I look back now it was a really good thing I put money in the bank. I planned ahead for myself.

Tony was gone, but I was still here. I would have been the one suffering if I had not ignored him and looked out for our later years. I created our pension. Though I rarely get credit for it, I am a smart person. I taught my sons how to save too, opening an account for them when they were young. I encouraged them to save part of the money they would get for birthdays and special occasions.

The people at the banks didn't believe I was married because they never saw Tony. They used to tease me asking if he was a real person. He had not thought about or planned for anything for the end of our lives. I had begged for years for him to go with me to make arrangements for our final resting places. I desperately needed to do this planning so that I could have a small bit of peace of mind.

But Tony did what Tony wanted to do. I told him it was later than he thought it was. He didn't listen to me, or anyone really. He was not a good listener. He bought really expensive hearing aids but would not wear them. When I got mad at him, I would tell him, "If I leave you, you will never find me." But even that threat never got him to do what I wanted him to do. He was always in charge. In my experience, that is pretty typical of Italian men born in Italy in that generation. He became an American fast. But like he used to tell the boys, "You see this piece of ground here (pointing to our property) this is MY Italy." They would try to reason with him about him not being in Italy anymore or try to get him to relax the rules because it was different in America. But this man, a good, loyal, honest and stubborn man, was not going to change.

We were a good team for the most part, especially when he had a project that had to be done and he needed my help. One winter the snow and wind had slid part of the roof on the business out of place. He had tried to get the boys to help him fix it. They said he needed a special machine for that. Tony and I went to the shop and he had me pumping up the jack that lifted the tilted section back in place. He loved telling me what to do, ordering me to move it a little more, then more still. I told him he was going to get us killed. He wanted to prove to the boys that this was no big deal, and no machine was needed to fix the problem. We got it done without any help from anyone else. Tony really was fearless.

Tony and me going out to dinner.

18-Capitolo Diciotto

One Thing After Another.

Retirement for my husband was a big adjustment for me. Tony had always been very controlling, but now it was worse because he was there all the time. For example, he informed me that I warmed my coffee in the microwave the wrong way. Imagine that!

Now, I have been drinking several cups of coffee every day, all my life, and I like it really hot. Tony only drank a half cup of coffee maybe once or twice a week. But he is telling me that after all these years, I was doing it wrong. Tony said I should put the handle of the coffee mug pointing towards me in the microwave and then set the time for an exact number of seconds that he had determined, and the mug handle would be pointing right at me when the microwave stopped. Then I could use the handle of the mug right there in front of me to take it out of the microwave. He honestly thought that was the best way to warm coffee and he expected me to do it that way. He was mad that I wouldn't. He even complained to my niece about me being unwilling to do it the right way. She told him she couldn't believe he was telling on himself like that! She said I could warm my coffee any way I wanted to. He said, "Oh you always agree with your aunt, you are always on her side."

He just didn't get it. Where the handle ended was not the point. It was how hot the coffee was. I had no trouble taking the mug out of the microwave, no matter where the handle of the mug ended up. I had been warming coffee all my life and I was not going to change just because he was home all the time now and watching my every move.

Tony was not well and was frustrated. It broke my heart watching him try to walk to his tool shed in the back yard with a cane in one hand and a crutch in the other. He moved so slowly, it took forever. Then he took to parking his riding lawn mower by the house so he could ride it to the tool shed. With his illness, he had let things go undone around the house. He didn't want the boys to do things, but he just was not able to do these things anymore.

Everywhere I looked there were important things that had needed to be done for months and years. We went without a doorbell. The fan over the kitchen table had a light dangling on the wire. The roof needed repair, the water softener filter was filthy, my basement kitchen needed a plumber…lots of things. So, as I cared for him, I watched the house go uncared for. That drove me crazy. He was my priority though.

The mess he left made me even madder at him after he was gone.

His desk, which he would not let anyone touch, had letters and statements from years ago. I have always been teased by him, the boys and others, about being a clean freak. My husband used to say, "I was born old with dirt in my eyes." I always kept a very clean house, so this was torture for me to see such a mess and then have to sort through all that after he passed.

Tony's smiling face that I used to talk to after he was gone.

I would look at his smiling picture and say some choice words in Italian to him when I was working on the mounds of papers and receipts he left behind. It was up to me to try to figure out what to save and what to shred. It was overwhelming.

He had gone to the hospital twice more since his heart surgery, but this last time he did not come home.

As I continue trying to come to

Sitting in my recliner in the family room.

terms with the loss, I never dreamed it would be this hard. I doze off in my chair and when I wake up, I expect to see him sitting there in his chair by me. The house is so quiet now. I listen for every little sound.

Our family room has two TVs, one on top of the other, so he could watch two games at once. I was used to him having both TVs going all the time. One would be turned up super loud, and the other one would be blaring in his ear on a headset that I could hear too. All those years working on cars had made him hard of hearing, but he would not wear his hearing aids. He would just turn up the volume on the TVs.

I'm sure I have hearing loss too, just from his TVs. Even though he was in no shape to protect me these last few years, just knowing he was there gave me a sense of security that I appreciated. I have never been alone like this before. I am extra careful now.

I had wanted a security alarm for our house, but my husband and sons decided on interior and exterior cameras. No alarm. I feel weird knowing they watch me. It is not what I wanted, but I am stuck with what those three had decided for me. It takes too much effort to fight them and I am tired.

Right after my husband died, my brother John and my sons were after me to get one of those life alert alarms since I was now living alone. I said okay, and I keep it with me so we all have some peace of mind. Right after I got it, I was wearing it around my neck like a pendant. I needed some potting soil for some strawberry plants I had ordered. I drove to my husband's favorite store, Home Depot, and picked up a ten-pound bag of soil and put it in my cart. I

My Life Alert before I tested it out.

was at the checkout, and I kept hearing a voice talking. I thought it must be my phone, so I started digging through my pocketbook for my cell phone. The girl checking me out said she thought it was a life alert alarm and asked me if I had one. I told her yes and looked down and sure enough, lifting that soil I had set it off and the voice was saying "Are you ok?"

I was embarrassed. I said, "I am fine. I must have bumped it when I picked up my potting soil." The people in line, the checker and the life alarm people all laughed at that. I couldn't figure out how the checker knew what it was. She told me her grandma had one just like it. Weeks later my son was over, and he said we needed to check the life alarm to be sure it is working. I told him it had already been tested. He went out to the garage to see how big the bag of potting soil was and then scolded me for picking it up. That is why I hadn't gotten around to telling him about it before then.

I don't wear it around my neck anymore. I keep the life alert in one pocket and my cell phone in the other.

When we retired, Tony had promised we would travel. Now he was gone. I still was interested in travel but didn't want to go alone. My American brother and his wife were celebrating their 65th anniversary one year after I lost my husband. There was a party with all his family from Kansas, Texas, Colorado and Missouri, all gathering together in Kansas, along with friends. I was invited.

Every letter my dad had written up until his death had included the question, "Why are you and your brother living so far apart?" Especially now I thought of that. With the urging and help

Me, my brother John, my sister-in-law Rosemary and my granddaughter Marie celebrating their 65th anniversary at their church in Kansas.

of my granddaughter, we added Pennsylvania to the list of five states to be in attendance, and we made the trip together. She was a pro at traveling, and she made sure it was a smooth and easy time for me. I was so glad I went!

It was good to see his kids and grandkids together in one place. I got to meet some new faces in the family for the first time, as two of his granddaughters had recently married. I hadn't been able to attend the weddings with Tony feeling as poorly as he did. Even my sister-in-law's sister's kids and grandkids, who call me Aunt Maria, were happy to see me. It warmed my heart to see everyone. I got so many hugs. My brother's friends were happy to see me too. What a great time my granddaughter and I had!

Making zeppole in my sister-in-law's kitchen.

We made *zeppole* the first night I got there. I had lots of help from my nieces and two of my great nieces in the kitchen. I wasn't used to that. It reminded me of being back home in Italy and baking and cooking in my mom's kitchen with my aunts and cousins. That was something I always missed about home.

We had so much fun. John's

I love cooking with family. This is Jeanmarie and her daughter Katy with me.

house was so loud with all the people talking and laughing. It was music to my ears, but some of those who married into the family (non-Italians) were bothered by all the noise. We ate and drank and the time just flew by. I hadn't been to Kansas in so many years. John had always told me to just come by myself if Tony wouldn't come. Well, I finally did come without him. That was a good thing to keep my mind on at the time of the first anniversary of his death. I was happy to be surrounded by people who loved me.

We got back home just weeks before the U.S.A. shut down.

We think we may have had a mild case of COVID 19 after flying home, as we were sick for a couple of weeks after that. But it wasn't too bad and we were still glad we went.

Just when I thought I had seen it all in my 92 years on this earth, here comes a pandemic! I lived through scarlet fever, the war, an earthquake, smallpox and so far, have survived living with E.T. I am also getting through reliving the war, because of the images on the news now from the war in Ukraine. That gives me bad dreams of being back in Moiano during the war.

The challenge of COVID 19 hit my Italy first and then came to my America. I am trying to be careful to stay away from the virus, for a bad case of that could be my end. With my age and being on chemo, I am considered a high-risk person for coronavirus. If I can avoid the virus, I guess E.T. is the sickness sent to take me to death.

Some days I don't know how I lived this long, but I am grateful for every day. Sunny, warm days are the best. I look at the flowers around my property that I have planted over many years. At my front door are two beautiful hibiscus plants with giant flowers all summer long. I pinch off spent blooms to keep it blooming. They make me smile. I love working in the garden. Up until last year, I still had a vegetable garden with tomatoes, string beans, cucumbers, peppers and asparagus. Over the years I have shared my garden harvest with many neighbors. I loved it when my grandkids were little, as they enjoyed my garden and would help me when they were over. It made me happy that they knew where vegetables came from and how they grew.

Being outside lifts my mood, but I have to be careful going out in the sun because of my chemo drug. It makes me more susceptible to sunburn and skin cancer. I am also very allergic to poison ivy. In the back yard I have a big chestnut tree that has good years and bad years for chestnut production. I have to race to beat the squirrels to them. They remind me of home, though I don't bury them in the dirt like we did when I was a kid. I vacuum seal them in a freezer bag. Then whenever I want some, I take them out of the freezer, cut an x in each one and then roast them toasty in the oven. That is an especially good treat for the holidays that I enjoyed in Italy.

Things I took for granted, like roasted chestnuts, were unknown to others here. They only knew of chestnuts from the song sung by Nat King Cole about "chestnuts roasting on an open fire" but had no idea what they looked like or how they tasted.

I have given up many of the other Italian holiday traditions now. I used to make *baccala* every Christmas eve, bake lots of Christmas cookies, make Easter bread, *zeppole*. I did my best to maintain the traditions I had grown up with so my sons and their families would appreciate their heritage. I gladly spent time showing others how to make Italian dishes so they could continue these after I am gone. So many times, I have shown people how to make sauce! It gives me great joy to make *cavatelli* with my grandson and his beautiful children.

19 – Capitolo Diciannove
As I Look Back.

The treatment by my relatives when I first came to this country still weighs on my heart. It is just so strange to me. I value relatives so much. I left nearly all of mine behind. I treasured my family and treated them well. I have forgiven those who mistreated us, but it is not forgotten. I had to learn to be tough and stand up for myself, but I had never had to do that with family when I lived in Italy.

When my aunt died, the one who had been so miserable to us, I made the three-hour drive to her funeral with my husband, my niece, and her husband. We paid our respects. I was always honorable. My parents taught me to be that way. I still have all the letters my dad wrote me when I was living with my aunt and uncle. They reinforce the respect that was required in my childhood home. We said hello to people who came over and called them by their titles, like Aunt *(Zia)* and Uncle *(Zio)*. In all my years I never let my parents down. I honored them by being that way. I am proud that I can say that.

I just keep celebrating birthdays.

I do not understand the lack of respect shown by some people today. Please and thank you *(per favore y grazie.)* Those spoken words remind us to always be grateful, every day, for what we have. When I got a thank you note from someone, it always made me smile. I appreciated the manners they were showing and was glad they had been taught manners. Some parents today do not seem to value that trait like us older people do. They either don't teach it or are unsuccessful at doing it. I do not blame the children. They must be taught.

Some days I wonder why I am still here. I look at young women today and see all they have, all they do, and wonder why they aren't happier with their lives. I always had to do what someone else told me to do, while they can make all their own decisions and do exactly as they like.

My mother and her sisters never got to go anywhere, not even school. They could not read or write. They were told they should not learn that because then they could have written to boys. It was very strict for girls. Three of my aunts lived on the same street and never left Moiano. The fourth sister lived her whole life in a nearby town. None of the girls went anywhere, but their brothers went to America. I got to go to school even though five years of school was all we had.

I think about it now and I can't believe how I did what I did. I surprised many, including myself. I went from a little girl named Maria who was afraid to ride a donkey, to an old woman named Mary with a car that automatically stops for me to avoid a collision. I didn't think I picked up things very fast, but I sure did well. My faith increased with each year. God helped me. The Black Madonna heard my many prayers. For a husband and wife team that could speak no English upon arrival, we achieved much.

I remember buying the World Book Encyclopedia set to have at home for the boys when they needed to research things for reports at school. It was really expensive, but we could not help them with their homework, so we wanted the books to help them. My husband said, "We will buy these books and send the boys to school. Then they will teach us." Today I cannot give away those books. No one wants them. It seems so wasteful to throw them in the trash, especially knowing how expensive they were, but that is what I have to do. Our World Books did their job; they taught our boys what we did not know about the world.

I was told I would go to America. I was told I was responsible for my brother in this new country, though I was just a kid myself. As I look back, I surprised myself that I did all this. How did I do all that I did? It is like a dream, like it was someone else.

I didn't get to choose, yet did well. I made the best of it, and I was happy with my life. When your back is to the wall you have to find a way. When you get in the water, you either swim or you drown. Sayings like that come to my mind.

I have had a good life. I have always treated people well. That makes me proud. My sons have made me very proud too. When the boys were in school, we finished the basement and put a pool table and fully stocked fridge down there for them and their friends. We welcomed their friends at our home and fed everyone well. We paid for our sons to go to all private schools: grade school, high school and college. They had no student loans to pay off upon graduation. They both have professional jobs, have done very well and will be prepared for retirement. Tony and I always did our best for them. I told them not to expect their wives to do things my way or to do all the things for them that I did for their father. We were from a different time and place.

My husband wished until the day he died that they would take over the business we had built together. That is the way it was done in Italy. One of our sons asked their dad why did we send them to college if he wanted them to take over the shop? My husband was wanting to do things the way he knew, the way things were in Italy. He wanted to continue some of the traditions of our birth country.

Our home and property had many remembrances of Italy, like

our "little boy" fountain we would drag out each spring for as long as we could lift it. It was a pretty little fountain on a pedestal, and it reminded us of Italy. But we lived longer in the U.S.A. than we did in Italy. We were citizens here, not in Italy. Our boys were Americans and did things their own way. I am glad I get to see my sons. They usually came for dinner once every week until the pandemic hit.

At my age, with all my experience, I thought I had seen it all. Then here comes a pandemic that spread from China through my home country to my adopted country. Really unbelievable!

I still feel fortunate to have lived to see my grandkids grow up into fine people that I am very proud of. My granddaughter is quite the traveler. She has been working on dual citizenship in the U.S. and Italy, with all the mounds of paperwork that go with that. My dad would have smiled at that. Just like him, with dual citizenship in the same countries.

My granddaughter Marie, who was named for me, and my niece Giuliana, who is Marie's godmother, with me after eating out.

My grandson and his wife blessed me with beautiful great grandkids to love as they begin their journey in this world. They are cared for so well and are a great joy in my life, always bringing smiles to my days. My iPad is where I see them mostly now, until things settle down. Yes, I have learned how to get face calls and see my great grandkids. I love seeing my relatives in Italy on the video calls. I can video call all by myself. Pretty good for a person in their 90s, can you believe it?

For Christmas 2020 we had a five-state Zoom call where I could see and hear 27 people, all at once. It was crazy. Who would have believed that could happen? Not me. It was amazing. It is so much better to see who you are talking to than just hear them on a regular phone call. I still can't believe that these video calls are free. It used to be you worried so much about how long you were talking on a long-distance call because of the bill that would be coming.

My family, in Italy and America…family is my favorite thing in this world.

My brother giving me a hug on a tough day.

20-Capitolo Venti

I Am Thankful.

I have had a good life. I learned respect and honor from my parents. My five years of school taught me to read and write in Italian. I learned to embroider from the nuns in Moiano. My Nonna taught me to knit. At the restaurant I learned to cook. A neighbor in Bristol, Mrs. Vigault, taught me to crochet. Elizabeth, who didn't drive, went with me to the store. She filled in as my American mom, helping me learn about my new country and helping me miss my mom a little less. Elizabeth was good company for me as a young mother. Every year we would make cookies for Christmas together. She began that tradition for me and I carried it on even now with my great grandkids. I was grateful to her for all these things and especially for giving my young sons someone to call grandmom in America.

I taught myself to clean and kept a spotless home for my family. I took great pride in my clean kitchen and home, even though people made fun of me about it. I taught myself English. America taught me to work hard, never give up and ignore those who made fun. I don't know how I survived it all. If someone had told me I was going to have to do all I did, I would have passed on the opportunity, that grand opportunity of going to America.

The choice was not mine, but I am proud of all I have learned and achieved. I am proud of being married for 66 years. I guess the rain on our wedding day was a good sign, but it certainly was not easy. My husband and I had our share of disagreements. It is called married life. One thing we disagreed on was this: If someone did something wrong, it was wrong, no matter who did it. There were not different rules for different people based on who they were.

I had friends who always agreed with their husbands, even when they were wrong, but I could not do that. That would be wrong. I also wanted the boys to know that the rules apply to everyone. My husband, of course thought that since he was my husband, I should agree with him. I stood my ground. I felt, as his wife, it was my duty to keep him honest and set a good example for our kids and grandkids. I also had to keep his superstitions under control. He was funny like that. He told me that things happened because I mentioned them. As if I could control the future!

This sign was put in our yard by a favorite new neighbor, Brenda, who did the design, delivery and photograph. The translation – A heart in love is always young.

If I could, I would have changed a lot of things. I was always looking ahead and playing it safe. I tried my best to be prepared for whatever was going to happen next. My husband was very annoying and controlling, but he was loyal and honorable. He earned the respect of this town where we made our home. He built a solid business where only rotten walls existed before. I was proud of what we did together, and I miss him a lot.

When we were first starting out in Bristol, we visited Emelia's brother in his new home. We got in the car to go to our apartment over the business and I said, "Emelia's brother, he did good." Tony asked me, "What do you mean?" I said, "They have a new house, a new Cadillac car and a baby." Tony told me he would order that for me. He would get that for me too. He would build me a

Taking a stroll with my niece Jeanmarie.

new house, buy me a new Cadillac and give me another baby. He did all those things. I wish I had a little more time with Tony.

Now that Tony is gone, the pestering is unbearable about when I will move from my home of over 60 years. I am glad I hadn't moved before the pandemic happened, as those places have been hit really hard by coronavirus.

It feels like people are waiting and watching for me to fail. It is not a good feeling. Sometimes I say things and people don't believe me just because I am old. It is so insulting. I am proud to say I have never treated the older people in my life that way. If I can remember my life's story like this, I am doing ok!

In my mind I have unfinished business. We started out with $2,000 in our pocket. Our business property that we bought for $27,000 was listed for sale at $600,000. I am proud to have been a big part of that success. Selling that and then my house needs to be completed, followed by the sale of the two extra lots we own behind our home. Only then will I really be ready for the final chapter in my life.

I have always chosen to do things in logical order, and I do not want to change that now. When I am ready, I will move. If one more person asks me when I am moving, I think I will hit them with my broom. My Nonna would be proud of me still using my broom!

Ciao!

Mary

Epilogue

After outliving all her lifelong friends in Bristol, my Aunt Maria reluctantly moved. She sold her business for the price she wanted. The realtor who represented the buyer called her and asked her how much she wanted for it. She told him and that was the price it sold for.

Mary in her independent living apartment.

Next, she put her house on the market and sold it for the price she wanted to a really nice couple. They love having her two kitchens. The wife uses the upstairs kitchen and the husband cooks in the downstairs kitchen. They gave her a tour of the house after they were settled in. They have visited her in her new home and continue to stay in touch with her. Mary is so happy that they appreciate the house she and Tony worked so hard to build with all the best things. My aunt misses Brenda and her husband, the neighbors next door to her house in Bristol, who did the anniversary sign. She enjoyed living by them. They have come to see her in her new place too. She is happy they have someone who is so nice living in her house as their neighbors.

Last of all, the two lots behind her house were sold at the price she wanted. She has been back to her old neighborhood to see the big, modern house they built there. Bristol has been a good place to live, and it still is. Just like Mary said, nearly every patch of ground available has been built on. The sales of their life's work ensures she never has to worry about money. She had met resistance about what the properties were worth. In true Mary style, she stuck to her opinion and she was proven right…three times. She knew the area well, and its value.

She is in independent living at a large retirement home in Pennsylvania that is more centrally located to her kids, grandkids and great grandkids. She is kind of famous there, as so many people know her. Mary has made many new friends who enrich her life and some are very dear to her. She has lost some good friends there, but is glad to have gotten to know them and spend time with them.

If you walk with her down the hall you have to try to keep up with her. Her "younger" brother was amazed at how quickly she walked and at all the "Hi Mary" greetings. Even after a fall that broke a leg and a wrist, Mary walks without a cane, walker or scooter, though many younger than her need them.

She continues to amaze people. One of her closest friends loves to challenge new residents to guess her age. No one can believe she is 96. She has taught people so much in her new place of residence. A friend in the sewing group was learning new crochet stitches from Mary, who was teaching the pattern from memory. Mary is also a popular invitee to dinner among the great group of people there. She treasures the time she spends with them, and the feeling appears very mutual. Friends are always offering to take her to the store or offering to help with anything she might need.

Though it has been many years and my aunt is far away, she has such a strong connection to her Italian hometown. When she sees pictures and videos on her iPad of the church and the festa of the Black Madonna in Moiano…it is like it was yesterday that she was there. It has happened many times that when new people meet her, they will ask her where she is from. She will say Bristol, Pennsylvania. Then they say, no, before Bristol, before that. She will usually laugh because she has been in Bristol much longer than she was in Moiano; in America, so much longer than Italy.

Author's Note

It was my honor to hear my Aunt Maria's story over many years and have her permission to put it down on paper, along with some of her recipes and kitchen tips.

This is her story, in her own words. She is an amazing, smart and beautiful woman. Starting in 1950, she courageously broke through barriers facing immigrants, especially women.

Mary conquered America and made it her home through extreme perseverance and hard work. This is a woman to be admired and respected...this girl named Maria.

Giuliana Palma

Giuliana at her wedding with her Aunt Maria and Uncle Tony.

A Girl Named Maria's Recipes and Kitchen Tips

Here are some of her favorites. She never wrote anything down; no written recipes, just her memory of how to do things.

CAVATELLI

My family eats this on special occasions.

2 pinches of salt

2 lbs flour

2 lbs ricotta

1 egg

Mix together in a bowl and knead until dough is ready. Add 2 teaspoons water if needed. Put a little flour down so it doesn't stick. Roll out the dough and stretch it to make dough finger thick. Cut into one finger wide long strips. Sprinkle a little flour on the machine and then feed strips into the cavatelli machine. Newly made cavatelli can be put into a pot of boiling water with a pinch of salt and cooked just like other pastas. If you want to freeze it and use it later, use cookie sheets covered with wax paper to put the cavatelli on in a single layer. Put the cookie sheets in the freezer and freeze. After frozen, remove from cookie sheets and put noodles in a freezer bag to be used when you want. Cook frozen cavatelli in boiling water with a pinch of salt until tender.

MOGLIAZZO

When I was young it was eaten for Easter with sweet bread.

1 lb spaghetti cooked al dente, drained and cooled

1 dozen eggs

½ lb Italian sausage cooked and chopped into small pieces

½ lb Mozzarella cut into small pieces

½ lb ham cut into small pieces

Beat eggs then pour over cooled spaghetti in large bowl. Add meats and cheese and mix together. Pour it all into 2 large skillets, either nonstick or with olive oil. Put on low heat and cover. When it is all jelled together and brown on the bottom, put a large platter on top of the skillet. Slide it out and then flip it over to brown the other side. Let it cool. Cut like a pie. Usually eaten cold but a slice can be warmed if preferred.

EASTER BREAD or PALOMMA or SWEET BREAD

Made for Easter, kids like the egg baked into the bread.

½ C lukewarm water	½ C butter
1 C light cream	1 ½ t salt
1 ½ C sugar	2 t vanilla
3 yeast pkgs	5 eggs
1 lemon - rind only, just the yellow part	5 ½ C flour

Stir yeast in lukewarm water. Set aside. Beat together butter and sugar. Add eggs and mix. Add rest of ingredients and work into dough form. Put in warm place and let rise one hour. Knead a little more and shape as you like for the bread, woven or braided in design along with 2 or 4 more uncooked, washed, and dried eggs in their shells if desired. Kids like that. Let rise in warm place for about an hour or until dough doubles in size. Bake at 350 for 35 minutes.

FENNEL TORALLI

I like to snack on these.

1 C lukewarm water

1 cake yeast

1 t salt

4 C flour

½ C olive oil

fennel seeds

½ t black pepper

Stir water, yeast and sugar together. Set aside. Put flour in large bowl then add the rest of the ingredients. Mix like macaroni, work the dough. When soft let rise in warm place. Then shape into pretzel or zeppole shape, press down to make it flat and let rise again. Bake in 400 oven for 10 minutes then lower oven to 350 until cooked.

MARIA'S CHICKEN NOODLE SOUP

I have been making this my whole life.

2 whole chickens cut into 4 pieces

4 onions cut into halves

a beef bone

3 good sized carrots

½ bunch of celery

fresh parsley

salt & pepper to taste

Fill a big pot with water. Then I tie the celery and parsley with string and dangle it on the side of the pot in the soup and put the beef bone in. Then I add all the other ingredients and cover. Bring to a boil then turn down to simmer, check regularly and remove foam that forms for a clear soup. Let simmer about an hour until chicken is done. Remove beef bone and chicken, debone the chicken and return to soup. Remove parsley and throw it away. Slice carrots, onion and celery; return to soup. When ready to eat soup, boil pastina pasta in separate pan according to package directions, drain and add to soup. Simmer a few minutes together then serve. Rice works too. Freezes well. Makes 10 quarts.

PIZZA PIENE

A family favorite.

For dough:
1C lukewarm water, ½ with yeast, ½ without yeast
3C flour
1 pkg yeast
Pinch of pepper
Salt to taste
1T Crisco to grease the pan

For filling:
½ lb slab bacon
½ to ¾ lb ham
1 supersade
1 brotsade sausage
1C grated Romano cheese
15 eggs
12 to 14 oz fine egg noodles

Dough – Mix all dough ingredients in a bowl. Work until it is the consistency of bread dough. Set dough aside in warm place and let rise for an hour.

Filling – Cook noodles according to package directions. Drain. Fry bacon. Finely chop ham, supersade, brotsade and bacon. Beat eggs together in a bowl. Add all the other filling ingredients to the eggs and mix well.

Dough – Split dough into 2 pieces. Take one piece and roll out to pie crust thickness. Grease a lasagna dish with Crisco and flour. Place rolled out dough in bottom and sides of lasagna dish just like pie crust.

Filling – Spread it evenly over crust.

Dough – Roll out other piece of dough and cover the top of the lasagna dish. Seal edges like a pie.

Bake at 350 for 2 hours.

ZEPPOLE

Made on Christmas and other holidays when we were all together.

2 ½ lbs potatoes – 1 part

7 ½ lbs flour – 3 parts

salt and pepper

yeast 3 or 4 pkgs dissolved in about 1 ½ C water room temperature

Take about 2 ½ pounds of potatoes, peeled and quartered. Boil in water with a teaspoon of salt. When potatoes are soft, drain well and mash. The amount of mashed potatoes you have, multiply that amount times 3 and that is roughly how much flour you will need. Let potatoes cool to room temperature. Use 3 or 4 packets of yeast for 2 ½ lbs. of potatoes. Mix yeast packets in 1 ½ Cups of room temperature water and let soak until doubled roughly.

Put the flour in large bowl and add yeast mixture then the mashed potatoes, salt and pepper to taste. Mix and knead into workable dough, can add warm water if needed. Turn out on minimally floured board and knead until soft. Put back in bowl and put a little olive oil on top to keep it moist. Let rise once in warm place until doubled. Turn out onto minimally floured board, punch down and roll out dough. Cut into strips, then cut strips to desired length, and make them into a loop or a little twist. Deep fry in olive oil, being sure to use as little flour as possible on the board as flour in the pan can burn. Take out of oil when golden brown and coat with granulated sugar, powdered sugar or cinnamon and sugar, whatever you like. Best eaten right away while hot.

EGGPLANT PARMIGIANA

I make this anytime I can find good eggplant at the store.

1 large eggplant

1 ½ C sauce, heated

½ lb mozzarella sliced thin

1 C fine bread crumbs

2 eggs slightly beaten

olive oil for frying

basil

grated parmesan cheese

salt and pepper

Wash eggplant and slice it thin. Stack slices in layers in colander lightly salting each layer. Repeat until all eggplant is done. Put a pot underneath colander. Cover eggplant with foil and put some weight on top of eggplant and leave overnight. In the morning pour water on top about 1 to 2 Cups and squeeze water out until dry. Use paper towels to dry out and get salty water out as best you can. Cover each slice with flour on both sides, followed by eggs then bread crumbs. Fry each slice in hot olive oil until tender and golden brown on both sides. Drain on paper towels. Line a shallow baking dish with sauce. Arrange a layer of browned eggplant slices over sauce followed by mozzarella, more sauce, basil and parmesan. Repeat until you are done with your eggplant slices. Bake at 350 for 25 to 30 minutes. May take longer depending on size of dish.

SPAGHETTI SAUCE

Chop onions then saute in olive oil with garlic. After onions are brown add a can of tomato paste. Stir together, saute for a few minutes. Add tomatoes. Italian plum tomatoes are best. Season with salt, pepper and other spices. If you want fine sauce, blend the canned tomatoes before using. Simmer sauce all day or as long as you want, stirring the bottom regularly to make sure it doesn't stick.

1 hour or 1 ½ hours before you are wanting to eat: put brasciole in sauce, leave them for a half hour in sauce, then add meatballs. Half hour later add sausage and let simmer all together - it is all ready for your cooked pasta.

BRASCIOLE

You will need: thin cut round steak, parsley, parmesan, garlic, salt, pepper.

Buy round steak sliced thin like for scallopini or ask butcher to slice it thin for you. Pound the steak thin and flat with a tenderizer hammer. Put salt, pepper, parsley, parmesan and garlic all over steak. Roll up with spices inside and tie with string or hold with toothpicks. Brown all sides in a skillet with hot olive oil.

MEATBALLS

You will need: pork, beef, dried day-old Italian bread cut into cubes like for stuffing, and eggs. For 5 lbs. of meat I use ½ loaf of bread.

I would buy a big pork roast and big beef roast and grind them at home and mix them together for my meat balls. If you do not want to do that just buy ground pork and ground beef. Mix meats together. Take the dried Italian bread crumbs and soak them in water. Squeeze out the water and then crumble the bread into the meat. Add 2 eggs per pound of meat used. Mix well. Form into meatballs and brown in pan with hot olive oil and brown on all sides.

SAUSAGE

I would buy good Italian sausage; boil it then drain. Brown all sides in hot olive oil. Add to the sauce with the meatballs. That gave my family 3 choices of meat with their pasta.

When I made meatballs and brasciole and sausage, I would make plenty so I could freeze some of each kind together in my food saver vacuum bags. Ready for a future meal.

Maria's Kitchen Tips

1) After draining your pasta, turn off the burner you just used and put your pan of pasta back on burner. Add a few ladles of sauce so that the sauce cooks into pasta and coats it well. Leave for a few minutes.

2) Save some of your pasta water to thicken your sauce as needed.

3) If there are holes in the center of your dough after cutting it with a knife, you have worked the dough enough. It is ready.

4) When coating meat or fish before frying, the order is flour, eggs, then crumbs. Use a section of saran wrap on a clean countertop for each one, then throw the saran wrap away when you are done for an easy clean up.

5) For clear broth remove any foam that appears when broth is boiling.

6) For broccoli or other greens add a pinch or two of baking soda to pan when cooking to retain their good green color.

About the Author

Giuliana (the Italian translation of her given name of Julianne) grew up in Topeka, Kansas where it was unusual to be Italian. Her father, Maria's brother, was the one the who was called if anyone in town needed an Italian to English translation. When her family visited her grandparents in Italy for the first time, it was front page news at the local paper. She was always proud to be Italian and took that cue from her Irish/English/German mother who was so proud of her Italian-born husband and his family.

Giuliana graduated from Washburn Rural High School and Washburn University in Topeka with a BA in Communications. She worked at three television stations and two newspapers before putting her photography and writing skills to work in her own freelance businesses. She is a member of the National Organization of Italian American Women (NOIAW), Italian American Writers Association (IAWA), and Kansas Authors Club. She is married to her high school sweetheart and they live in Leawood, Kansas. They have a beautiful daughter.

A Girl Named Maria is Giuliana's first book.

Giuliana Palma

BooksByGiuliana@gmail.com

BooksBy Giuliana on Facebook

JPIrelandPhotography@gmail.com

www.ingramcontent.com/pod-product-compliance
Ingram Content Group UK Ltd.
Pitfield, Milton Keynes, MK11 3LW, UK
UKHW060126010826
14089UKWH00023B/269/J

9 798992 767087